THE INTERNATIONAL CONTEXT OF

RURAL POVERTY

IN THE THIRD WORLD

THE INTERNATIONAL CONTEXT OF
RURAL POVERTY
IN THE THIRD WORLD

Issues for Research and Action
by Grassroots Organizations
and Legal Activists

International Center for Law in Development

Edited by

David Dembo
Clarence Dias
Ward Morehouse
James Paul

Council on International and Public Affairs
New York

Published by the
Council on International and Public Affairs, Inc.
in Cooperation with the
International Center for Law in Development
777 United Nations Plaza
New York, NY 10017

1986

ISBN 0-936876-40-9

PREFACE

This volume grows out of the continuing concern of the
International Center for Law in Development with legal,
political, and other obstacles to equity-enhancing, participatory development in the Third World. While we hesitate to
claim uniqueness, we believe the collection of reports in
the pages following is distinctive in examining critically
several of the major international forces which adversely
affect the poor in the name of "development."

These various forces--transnational agribusiness and
the international trading system, so-called "modernization"
of food systems, international development agencies, advanced technologies and food "aid" from the First World,
etc.--have often been analyzed separately from one another.
We have sought here to bring together the perspectives and
insights of the several contributors to this volume in an
effort to understand how these forces converge on the rural
poor in the Third World. The final chapter seeks to draw
lessons for action from the preceding chapters in using
human rights and legal resources to combat rural impoverishment.

We should like to express our appreciation to the contributors to this book. It is truly the case that the volume

could not have appeared without them, nor would it have
appeared when it did without their cooperation in revising,
and in more than one instance, revising again their draft
manuscripts at the request of the editors. We should also
like to thank Cynthia T. Morehouse for copy-editing the man-
uscript and Helen Ko for enduring what must have often
seemed to her a never-ending process in producing the camera
ready copy from which this book has been printed.

We hope the volume will help to raise awareness among
grassroots organizations of the rural poor regarding some
of these international forces which constrain the effectiveness of their own efforts in combating impoverishment and in
striving toward participatory, self-reliant development. We
also hope it will be useful to legal activists and others in
support action groups concerned about the problems created
by these international forces which affect the poor in less
visible and often more intractable ways. Only by understanding clearly the nature and causes of such a complex and difficult problem as rural poverty in the Third World is it
possible to mount a meaningful attack on that problem.

New York   David Dembo
February, 1986   Clarence Dias
                                                Ward Morehouse
                                                James Paul

CONTENTS

I. INTRODUCTION

Editors' Note

LEGAL RESOURCES TO COMBAT
RURAL IMPOVERISHMENT

Since its inception ICLD's concerns have centered on
those who are the primary "victims" of underdevelopment and
maldevelopment in the Third World: the rural poor who constitute the vast majority of people in most Third World
countries. In some settings these concerns focus on the
victims of various kinds of social relations which help per-
petuate impoverishment and impotence--such as exploitative
systems of land tenure, employment, moneylending, or marketing. In other settings the focus is on the victims of historic official neglect and discrimination in the allocation
of essential services (such as health care and education).
In still other settings the focus is on the victims of "development" policies and programs which may benefit some
sectors of society but at great cost to many others--for
example, projects to impose dams, plantations, or large-
scale commercial farming projects on rural environments.
All too often these kinds of projects create whole new
classes of landless families and marginal wage workers--and
new forms of indebtedness, dependency, and poverty.

In most of these settings the lot of these kinds of
victim groups is also characterized by lack of power--
including lack of power to use and develop law to protect

their rights. If these rights are to be protected, victim groups must be helped to develop "legal resources"--a functional knowledge of relevant law and the skills to <u>use</u>, and <u>develop</u>, law in order to promote and protect shared group interests and rights. ICLD works with other organizations to aid this process.

Legal resources are, of course, only part of the resources which these organizations need; but the generation of group capacities to use law is often quite important. When groups enjoy legal resources they enjoy capacities to understand law and to assert rights and win their recognition. Plantation workers and sharecroppers can claim protections provided by legislation dealing with wages and other conditions of employment, and they can demand recognition and enforcement of such protections where they do not presently exist. Small farmers can organize collective activities to secure more effective access to credit, markets and, inputs. Communities can organize schemes to develop self-managed health care facilities, water resources' projects, and other services, and they can press claims on governments to aid these projects. When people enjoy legal resources they can challenge, more effectively, those activities which threaten them with landlessness or other impoverishing economic relations, or which threaten the quality of their physical and social environments.

This volume is intended as a modest contribution to the struggles of organizations, in many parts of the world, to develop legal resources which will help the victims of various kinds of international development schemes to fight back--to seek redress of harms inflicted upon them by those who impose these schemes on rural communities.

The first purpose of the volume is to present reports which focus on <u>impoverishing practices and conduct</u> of participants in international development schemes (e.g., the World Bank and other international organizations, multinational corporations and their local surrogates, state, and parastatal agencies in "host" countries). We seek to show how these "development" actors engage in conduct--or openly condone conduct--which inflicts impoverishing harms on rural people <u>and</u> which is unlawful because it violates the legal rights of those so seriously wronged. Thus, some reports in this volume highlight wrongful practices used to wrest land from cultivators in order to build dams or create corporate plantations. Others show how small farmers are pressured into the production of new crops coupled with contractual arrangements which ensnare families into new cycles of indebtedness. Others depict different kinds of exploitative employment relationships which so often accompany development of various kinds of enterprises. Several papers describe the harms threatened by the international "food aid" programs, or by the introduction of new technologies in agriculture, notably new biotechnologies.

Efforts to prevent and redress conduct which causes these harms must include efforts by victim groups and those working for them. In most settings it is simply unrealistic to hope that these wrongdoers (notably, governmental and public international agencies) will, by themselves, come to recognize and respect the rights of persons threatened by development projects. Victim groups must, themselves, fight for recognition of their rights. Thus, a second purpose of the volume is to outline, illustratively, some strategies which these organizations may wish to pursue, in <u>their</u>

struggles for empowerment, equitable treatment, and development.

While there is, of course, an extensive literature on the dislocation effects of the transnationalization of Third World economies, little has been written from the perspective of the concerns underlying this volume--the need to help victims fight back. We hope this work may make some contribution toward the development of these efforts and the development of the rights of victim groups and remedies to enforce them.

LAW, STRUGGLE, AND CHANGE IN INDIA:

AN AGENDUM FOR ACTIVISTS

Upendra Baxi

While this essay is focused on law and
social change in India, it has varying
degrees of relevance to other Third
World countries, where social action
groups have in the past viewed the law
only as an instrument of repression
and are now beginning to explore its
potential for emancipation of the poor.

The Editors

The Propagation of Limits of Law

The burgeoning literature on the relations between law
and social change celebrates the limits of effective legal
action. Much of this literature comes from the First World.
The Indian outpourings on the subject thrive on pilfered
phrases and pale impersonations of and borrowed wisdom from
First World articulations. Law persons (and occasionally
social scientists) keep on telling lay persons in India that
the law cannot lead change but can only follow it, that it
cannot be an instrument of basic transformation of values
and attitudes, and that there are other agents of social
change far more crucial than law. An ideological climate is
thus created to devalue the role of law.

Everyone, including the activists and social action
groups (SAGs), are made to understand the limits of law even

before they understand its potential to foster directed social change. An important task on the agenda of social activists and SAGs in contemporary India is to understand how law, as it *exists today*, can be used in favor of the exploited classes and against the dominant ones.

For this to happen, activists and SAGs will have to combat their own internal ideologies which assign the most marginal place to state law. Among the more entrenched people's groups in India are the Gandhian or neo-Gandhian, the Marxist, and the liberal ones. The Gandhian or neo-Gandhian groups inherit a world view in which the moral integrity of the individual and the collective ethic of a group remain the vital forces for social transformation. Struggle against domination has to be peaceful and punishment for knowing violation of the law has to be borne with dignity. The state law is external to conscience; over-reliance on it is, therefore, against the development of ethical sensibility as a prime mover for social transformation. The "left-wing" groups regard the state law primarily as an instrument of class oppression. By definition, then, an activist assertion cannot rely on state law and its processes. To do so will be to enhance the legitimacy of the state and its law which must be challenged and exposed by social action. Perhaps the purest form of radical groups' approach to state and the law is to be found in Naxalite "jurisprudence" which believes in the creation of alternate legality (people's courts, public executions of the "enemies of the people," terror as distinct from structured coercion as the basis of legitimation of a new polity), and in the annihilation of state law and its agencies and agents.

In contrast, the liberal groups, whose presence is now

growing, believe in sustained or episodic and opportunistic strategic uses of the law. The liberal NGOs are marked by their metropolitan locations and decision-making leadership and by a high presence of NGIs (non-governmental individuals), such as academics, lawyers, retired justices, and administrators. Other liberal groups, not having a metropolitan location or such professional leadership, are in the habit of activating law (mostly within courts) when they can or when they must. But for those operating at the grass-roots, access to the law, the aftermath of its activation, and the future impact of the use of law on their leadership and organization continue to present rather constant dilemmas in their struggle.

As the reader would realize, this classification of activists and groups is by way of ideal types; in real life, one finds mixed types. One also notices tendencies in real life toward transition from one category to another. For example, the essentially Gandhian-oriented organizations of the rural poor (like the Rangpur Ashram led by Harivallabh Parekh or the Chipko movement) have become "liberal," at least insofar as their approach to the law is concerned, and left-oriented groups do use the courts rather effectively (e.g., the Lawyers' Collective or the PUDR). But the essential ideology concerning the role of the law in social transformation is not drastically changed in the process; the law is only used tactically and strategically, while the overall negation of the law remains latent as the basic theoretical approach.

The Rule of Law and the
Reign of Terror

Activists and groups encounter law typically at its
repressive worst. They thus internalize the fact that law
is the negation of freedom and justice and the very embodi-
ment of arbitrariness and cruelty. More concretely, the law
to the poor means suffering the lawlessness of the agents
and institutions of the state and of law. I may be arrested
without any reasonable ground for suspicion; handcuffed or
roped like an animal and taken to the police station without
a word of explanation; locked up, beaten, and sadistically
tortured at the whim of the captors; produced before the
magistrate at the will of the captors; put in jail for years
on end without judicial proceedings even beginning; and made
to slave in jail without wages and, if young, bartered for
homosexual relations. Or, my wife and daughter may be raped,
my hut set ablaze, my small belongings looted or destroyed
by the militia of the landlords or para-military forces of
the state. Or, I even might be shot dead in "encounters"
and posthumously proclaimed as a "dacoit," "extremist," or
"Naxalite."

This is clearly a part of the reality of the state law.
The law may create, in Karl Marx's words, "circumstances of
reckless terrorism" and display a "purely *policemaniac* character in dealing with the subjugated 'classes.'" When the
state law assumes a policemaniac character, it also mani-
fests the tendency of the state toward lawlessness. The
normative law of the state prohibits standardless use of
force; reign of terror is nothing but that. Terror, therefore, involves organized illegality by state agents. In
this sense, the state is inherently lawless. Or, to put it

in another way, "every state is organized as a single functional order of legality and illegality" (Nicos Poulantzas, *State Power and Socialism*, 1982, p. 85). There is, thus, no way of saying that *law does not exist as a reign of terror.*

At the same time, law also exists *as the rule of law* and this reality also cannot be denied. It is this ideology which provides the principle that distinguishes between the lawful and the unlawful uses of force and enables us to distinguish "terror" from "legitimate force." It is the rule-of-law ideology which prescribes that wherever there is power, there is accountability--that the two cannot be divorced. It is this ideology which campaigns against arbitrary exercise of state power and gives us values, such as formal and substantive equality and freedom. Not merely this. It provides an ensemble of structures and institutions within which these precepts could be continually elaborated, entrenched, and enforced *against the state.*

Thus, the state law is a contradictory social reality. It is, according to Marxian analysis, the very task of the rule-of-law ideology to mask the reign of terror. But terroristic repression cannot be masked as far as the immediate victims of repression are concerned, nor for those who struggle on behalf of the victims. In any case, unmasking is only possible if the rule-of-law ideology exists in the first place. Where it does not exist, bullets (from both sides) are the only argument. You do not invoke reasoned arguments appealing to standards of justice in the face of such regimes of terror as those of Adolf Hitler, Idi Amin, or Papa "Doc." To be an activist in such regimes is also to be a terrorist, and the best strategy is what medievalists called "tyrannicide" and modern wisdom describes as a "coup."

At the present stage in societies like India, what we have is a *co-presence* of terror with the ideology of the rule of law. In such a situation, the state law can be effectively used to expose the state's lawless terror. It can also be used to combat repression. It may be relatively harder for people's groups to wield the rule-of-law ideology as effectively for emancipation as it is used by the dominant groups for repression. But it is possible to use and enhance the liberational profile and content of the law as legislation, adjudication, and administration. State law provides ideologies, institutions, and structures which can be effectively used for domination as well as in struggles against domination.

ORPs, PORPs, and SAGs Defined

People's groups--Organizations of the Rural Poor (ORPs), Participatory Organizations of the Rural Poor (PORPs), and Social Action Groups (SAGs)--are classified into these three categories in this paper for the sake of convenience, rather than out of any theoretical mischief. The key distinction here is between ORPs and PORPs. ORPs do not adopt participation as a principle of organization; PORPs do precisely this. Among the ORPs, we include a whole variety of groups-- party-based cadres, non-party developmental groups (e.g., Rangpur, Chipko, Tilonia); specific constituency groups (e.g., environmental groups, women's organizations, caste upliftment associations); mobilization groups (e.g., Chhattra Vahinis; and task-oriented service groups (Jyoti Sanghi, Sanjeevini, Nari Rakshakamitis, or anti-dowry groups). PORPs include such participatory ORPs as the Bhoomi Sena and Kastakari

Sangathana.

SAGs present a wide variety of activities. Essentially, SAGs are linkage and service groups; they are designed to assist ORPs and PORPs in normal times as well as in distress. Mostly, they are city-based and managed by members of ideological professions, including the social science establishment. They seek to understand ORPs and PORPs through dialogical research, and to serve ORPS and PORPs through:

a) fostering communication and coordination among diverse groups within the region and across the nation;

b) creating and mobilizing upward linkages of power and influence in support of ORPs and PORPs;

c) providing orientation, evaluation, and self-correction mechanisms to ORPs and PORPs; and

d) providing specialized services and skills (such as legal advice).

The SAGs category would include such entities as PIDT (People's Institute of Development and Training); Lokayan; Rajpipla Free Legal Services Programmes; CERC (Consumer Education and Research Centre); Gandhi Peace Foundation; ASSALT (Association for Social Action and Legal Thought); PUDR (People's Union for Democratic Rights); and PUCL (People's Union for Civil Liberties).

Some Experiences of the
Liberational Uses of State Law

Many ORPs, PORPs, and SAGs encounter in the early phase

of their organization and activities a disproportion between their knowledge of the repressive procedures and contents of state law and the liberative contents of the state law. They have sure knowledge of the varieties of repressive experience that the state law promises and provides, but little information about the liberational potential of the self-same state law. This cognitive gap is *not* accidental. It is structured in the very mode of production of the state law. The mode of production of the state law *determines* the level of legal illiteracy and ignorance. The state law is so produced that its beneficiaries may have the least prospect of knowing about it. This applies not just to the legislative law but also to judicial law.

Be that as it may, groups of and for the rural poor often cannot use the law as a resource to combat excesses of power because of the well-nurtured incidence of legal ignorance. But when this ignorance is removed, howsoever slightly, the groups gain in strength.

The knowledge that the crop-protection society militia, maintained by the landlords, is not equivalent to state police has proved useful--even important--to the Kastakari Sangathana. ORPs, dealing with the landless poor, often find it exceedingly useful in their struggle with landlords for just wages to know the precise rates of minimum wages under the Minimum Wages Act. The Chipko movement was aided by information concerning certain constraints on the forestry and revenue bureaucracy upon their ability to award licenses for the felling of trees. Information about debt-relief legislation enabled *Adivasis* (tribals) of Rangpur villages to accomplish massive scaling of debts and to even seek their cancellation. Information about the impending

introduction of a forestry bill in India, which created a
very large variety of forest offences--including those of
unauthorized removal of grass and leaves--has already enabled concerned groups to successfully energize the public
opinion of a large number of Adivasis throughout the country.

Undoubtedly, access to legal information diminishes to
some extent or other the vulnerability of the poor to exploitation or manipulation. It also introduces possibilities of change in power relations between the people and
their adversaries, as well as considerably fostering the
processes of self-reliance and self-assertion.

But access to legal information can have other beneficial impacts on the internal structure and function of the
people's groups themselves. The internal constitution of a
people's group may, at times, be assisted by the models of
organization provided by state law, such as credit cooperatives, registered societies, trusts, trade unions, companies, and partnerships. Most people's organizations tend to
operate outside these organizational models; in a sense,
they do not exist as entities in the eye of the state law.
But often this happens because ORPs have no real information
on the relative merits of alternate organizational forms
under state law.

The point about these models is that they provide the
accumulation of legal experience for structuring associa-
tional or group activities. What is more, these models provide essentially facilitative, non-coercive, legal arrange-
ments--and they provide a wide range of choice. It goes
without saying that any ORP needs some norms for internal
structures, and functional spontaneity is just not enough.
There arises a need for certain norms, tacit or explicit,

governing decision making, allocations of tasks and benefits, management of affairs, recruitment and training of
cadres and personnel, and accountability of active leaders
to the rank and file. ORPs not only need to have an internal constitution; they should also be imbued with their own
distinctive spirit of constitutionalism.

This way of expressing the need for internal constitution for ORPs, of course, states the matter too formally but
it indicates at least the broad range of problems arising
for ORPs, PORPs, and SAGs. Sooner or later, at some point
of their development, a choice is made of a legal form.
Some SAGs start with an explicit choice--SEWA, the Self-
Employed Women's Organization, or PIDT, the People's Institute of Development and Training. (The former is a trade
union registered under the law, while the latter is a registered society.) Some ORPs and PORPs who defer these choices
later find themselves in a situation requiring a choice.
Sometimes the need for choice arises out of the nature of
the enterprise preferred by an ORP. For example, an ORP
decides to sell its produce not to the local trader who
offers a low price but to an outside trader. This marketing
arrangement may entail a common fund which has to be admin-
istered to everyone's satisfaction and benefit. Appropriate
information concerning the range of legal forms which facilitate ORPs is indeed vital.

Aside from this *constitutive* role of legal information,
we may also find that information about the state law often
helps ORPs to fashion more effective strategies for the at-
tainment of social change objectives over a period of time.
If state law imposes prohibitions on the reckless felling of
trees or the pollution of environment, or provides for free

and compulsory education of children or family planning services, the ORPs, following the same objectives, can attain several concrete results by using the same informational guidelines. First, they can resist delegitimization from adversaries by stressing the commonality of the developmental objectives. Second, they can negotiate bureaucratic contingencies more effectively--from obtaining major resource allocation decisions in their favor to even getting support for such a seemingly small step as the use of a public place in a village for a night school for landless laborers (at the same time, obtaining a priority quota for kerosene lamps for this purpose from the public distribution system). Third, ORPs can, by reference to the commonality with the national objectives embodied in the state law, add to their capabilities to withstand repression. Fourth, ORPs can also obtain thereby political space and time--both valuable resources in themselves--needed for their growth and viability. Last, but not least, insofar as ORPs are funded (especially from overseas), they need to have a legitimate name, operational base, and a bank account. The process of acquiring these is facilitated by invocation of commonality.

The question of effective access to law is vital to people's groups. But it should not be regarded as merely a problem of information. The problem of information is also one of power and domination. People's groups have to consider alternatives to the present mode of production of state law, including participative law making, interpretation, and enforcement. Episodic liberational uses of the law will relate primarily to the problem of access. Sustained liberational strategies will question, and delegitimize, the systemic creation of legal ignorance.

*Recourse to Law or to Direct
Action*

The ORPs' legal consciousness will also determine the
range of the uses of law which may be imaginatively built
into social action as well as cadre-building and training
programs. If the ORPs are opportunistic and casual law
users, the liberational potential of the law is likely to be
overlooked. This may happen in a variety of important ways.

The ORP may overlook the choices made available by the
legal system in planning its strategies. The system might
provide a simple and effective remedy through court activation (say an injunction) as against a prolonged and taxing
campaign of direct action or civil disobedience. Of course,
while the primary aim of direct action is to politicize consciousness, recourse to courts tends usually to have the
opposite impact. But direct-action strategies, if consistently overused, make demands on leadership and constituents
that eventually may make such direct action counter-productive.. Most ORPs have not been able to evolve the right mix
of recourse to law and direct action. To that extent, either they have been ineffective in some of their campaigns
or they have achieved success at high costs of enervation.
Fasting up to death--*gherao*, which literally means encircle-
ment of the adversary until a decision is revised--picketing,
processions, marches, all involve gains of mobilization, participation, publicity, and politicization. On the other
hand, they also might involve considerable leadership and
economic costs. Direct-action modalities may also occasionally involve survival costs (as when police use riot control
methods and even shoot on sight), freedom costs (as when
large numbers of people are arrested and detained), and

dignity costs.

The gains of successful direct-action campaigns are, of course, always impressive, but when a campaign fails, the costs appear no less striking. And overuse of strategies may so routinize direct action as to deprive it of its symbolic mass protest value; they indeed become political rituals which hard-nosed administrators regard as being no more than a routine order of business at best (in terms of response or repression), or as occupational hazards at worst.

ORPs frequently do not realize that direct action is made possible only because the legal system provides for free expression of dissent through organized public gestures. If the law and polity did not tolerate collective peaceful protest and was inhospitable to even the most innocuous expression of organized public opinion, people's groups would be deprived even of this much political space.

If this is fully grasped, the choice of strategies between direct action and the recourse of law is not between legal and non-legal action. Both are law-related actions. Both have their manifest and latent costs and gains. Both involve exercises in political rationality. The antithesis is not really between direct action and recourse to courts; it is rather between an effective and ineffective strategy in certain specific contexts.

Of course, it may be extremely difficult for most ORPs to identify certain problems as those which may be met by simple recourse to law. The poor typically fail to identify their problems as distinctively legal and indeed not many could really be so identified. This understandably gets carried over to organizations of the rural poor. But alternate legal modes of action do enhance the capabilities of

ORPs, and ways have to be found to carry this message to them.

Legal Activism and Social Action
Litigation

Access to information is only a part of the story; access to favored interpretation of state law by the ORPs and PORPs is another. And access to interpretation, preeminently by recourse to courts and tribunals, is also a form of domination and power. In a sense, the power to interpret laws is the power to make them, and the power to manipulate the interpretation process is also the power to make law. But the interpreters and manipulators of interpretation, lawyers and judges, are themselves not easily accessible to the poor or the ORPs. Part of the reason for their non-availability is, of course, the class character of the legal profession and the judiciary. But a part of the explanation lies also in the fact that the poor and the ORP do not provide any systematic input of their problems in the court system in a proactive manner. And the reason for this lies in the divergent legal consciousness of the ORPs and PORPs! Once again, through this vicious circle the people's groups lose whatever opportunities they have of activating the liberational potential of the state legal system.

This deadlock can be broken only by the initiative of legal SAGs. Unless legal activists emerge, the gulf between courts and poor must remain almost the same. And the emergence of legal activists, whether academics, lawyers, or judges, is itself problematic and contingent. India has witnessed its first real upsurge of legal activism (even among justices of the Supreme Court) only in the past four years.

This can be explained by the catharsis of middle and upper middle classes, and their slight radicalization in the period following the return to parliamentary rule in 1977 after the internal Emergency.

Social action litigation in India has emerged through uncoordinated use of law by scattered legal activists in the universities, the bar, the bench, and the media. The following episodic review indicates the range and scope of present developments:

-- Four law professors issued an open letter to the Chief Justice of India, sharply criticizing its decision acquitting police constables accused of committing rape of a tribal woman within the confines of a police station on the specious ground that because she did not resist she must have consented to sexual intercourse. This created a nationwide controversy, led swiftly to a bill proposing an amendment of the criminal law relating to rape, and a protest march by women's organizations to the Supreme Court seeking a review of the decision.

-- The Supreme Court of India, acting on complaints by or on behalf of prisoners, has revolutionized, normatively at least, prison jurisprudence.

-- Journalists have sought intervention of the Court to prevent the buying and selling of women (the Kamala case), the torture of Naxalites in Madras jails, and the importation for carnal use of children in a Kampur prison. They have also called for a full investigation into extra-judicial investigation of police "encounters" with dacoits which have resulted in extra-judicial executions of people in the rural areas of Indian states.

-- Public-spirited lawyers have questioned
   with remarkable success the long incarceration of people awaiting trial for crimes
   carrying maximum sentences, often under
   half the period of pretrial detention already served.

-- A Bombay-based lawyer group has persuaded
   the Supreme Court to admit a petition
   claiming that pavement dwellers in Bombay
   have a fundamental right under the Constitution to dwell on pavements and has filed
   a writ claiming access to clean and hy-
   gienic drinking water for villagers in
   Maharashtra.

-- An agonized Supreme Court is proceeding to
   fix culpability for the blinding of under-
   trials in Bihar and has ordered a number
   of compensatory measures.

-- Two law professors have filed writ proceedings for violation of constitutional rights
   of women detained in a protective home for
   women in Agra and for cruel and sadistic
   torture of eleven young persons in Madhya
   Pradesh jails.

-- A legal sociologist has successfully moved
   the Court to secure expeditious trial of
   four boys under detention for seven to
   eight years for a crime they did not com-
   mit.

The Supreme Court has also assumed an activist role.
It has developed a simple and swift technique of what must be
called "epistolary." SAGs and bona fide public citizens may
simply write a letter to a judge of the Supreme Court or High
Court, concerning excesses of public power against the deprived and the dispossessed, and the Court will treat it as
a writ petition. The rules on *locus standi* have been radically liberalized to allow this and associated forms of

action. The Supreme Court and the High Courts have appointed socio-legal commissions of inquiry to ascertain facts. Courts have also assumed *suo motu* jurisdiction to review lawless use of force by agents of the state. Compensation for violation of fundamental rights is now emerging as a new constitutional principle. The lawlessness of the state stands massively exposed and indicted.

For the first time India has a National Committee on the Implementation of Legal Aid Programmes (as distinct from committees on legal aid which produce excellent blueprints of what needs to be done). Aside from the routine dispensation of legal services through state boards, the committee has started a unique program of legal aid camps. These camps are held in rural areas where specific collective complaints of the rural poor are attended to in the presence of Supreme Court and High Court judges, district judiciary, administration, and police. Some of these camps have been held at the request of an ORP.

This is an unprecedented and remarkable development quite likely to survive the reactionary onslaughts against it by those who were accustomed to the use of judicial process only by the privileged few to protect *their* interests and values. The future of social action litigatiuon is indeed quite bright. Already many ORPs have begun to realize the potentialities of the liberational uses of law, and not a week passes without at least one group trying to reach out to legal activists for initiation of social action litigation on behalf of the poor.

Social Action Litigation:
Prospects and Limits

Among the gains of social action litigation are: the
heightened sensitivities to injustice on the part of a
cross-section of the elite; accountability of the ruling
classes and dominant political institutions; a gradual, pro-
people renovation of judicial process and values; emergence
of a special kind of confidence in the judiciary in its unequal battle with administrative deviance; and a crystalli-
zation of informed consensus on the need for fundamental reform of the legal system. Given the unplanned efforts of a
few individual legal activists, with shoestring budgets and
poor infrastructural facilities, these achievements are indeed astonishing.

However, first we must note that courts may not rever-
berate with such populism every time and everywhere. Even
the Indian experience is somewhat unique in terms of the history of adjudication in the country. But it highlights the
fact that just judges everywhere are sensitive human beings
who can be made to understand and appreciate the repressive
potential and reality of the law, and that they can be converted into crucial resources for legal mobilization.

Second, we have to acknowledge that court recourse means
depoliticization of the problem. The bonded laborers may be
freed by a judicial order, but the social meaning of liberation and its political message for the structure of power relations may well be lost.

Third, even when we activate judicial power to combat
legal repression, we may acknowledge constantly that the
limits of social action litigation are the very limits of law
and legal action. Such action removes constraints on liberty

by eliminating repression, but it does not provide conditions which would make the restoration of liberty meaningful. Persons detained over ten years or more, awaiting
trial, may be set free, but how can legal activists help
them to stand on their feet after all the enormous disadvantages attendant upon incarceration? Bonded laborers may be
freed from debt bondage, but what can social and legal activists do to help them realize the full meaning of their
liberation? To what extent can courts be asked to fashion
lasting and meaningful measures of relief that would add
meaning to the endowment of freedom? How far may courts
compel the state to atone concretely for lawlessness of the
law? How do courts and legal activists monitor institutional reforms compelled by social action litigation? How
can one structurally lessen, through judicial intervention,
administrative deviance and governmental lawlessness? How
does one overcome the bureaucratic contingencies involved in
realizing the full ameliorative import of such measures of
relief and rehabilitation as courts may be persuaded to
grant?

To raise at random some of these problems is to raise
again the problem of the legal consciousness of the PORPs,
ORPs, and SAGs. Unless they develop a *systemic* interest in
the state law and *campaign* as a part of their action for
emancipation of the poor, massive invocation of the social
action jurisdiction will lead to widespread disenchantment
in the coming years. Such an agenda for action would include:

a) reform of the administration of justice;

b) increase in the strength of judges and
    level of their social commitment;

c) reorganization of the colonial police
force into a democratic people's police
force;

d) effective prosecutorial staff and practices;

e) simplicity and clarity in legal drafting
and greater participation of people's
groups in the drafting process;

f) humanization of penal and correctional
institutions;

g) greater social accountability of the legal
profession;

h) effective participative procedures for law
reform; and

i) right to access to information.

Without some progress on this agenda, the underlying
structure of legal institutions and processes will remain
unaffected by social action litigation and very few ORPs,
PORPs, and SAGs will have the capabilities to back up and
oversee the implementation of judicial directives. Social
action litigation will then begin to be perceived as only a
symbolic leverage for a more just and responsive social order. Unless the liberational potential of the law is enhanced *as a part of the struggle* for emancipation of the
poor, the repressive reality will continue to haunt them with
all its diabolical force. Herein lies the challenge of law
to social action.

References

Baxi, Upendra, "Taking Suffering Seriously: Social Action Litigation Before the Supreme Court," *Delhi Law Review*, Nos. 8 & 9, 1979.

_____, *The Indian Supreme Court and Politics*, Lucknow: Eastern Book Company, 1980.

_____, *The Crisis of the Indian Legal System*, Delhi: Vikas Publishing House, 1982.

_____, "The Law as Terror and the Law as Idealogy: 'Force Without Phrases' and 'Force of Phrases'" in Baxi, editor, *Marx Law and Justice*, Bombay: N.M. Tripathi, forthcoming 1986.

Nicos Poulantzas, *State Power and Socialism*, London: Verso, 1980.

II. "TRANSNATIONALIZATION" OF THIRD WORLD AGRICULTURE

TRANSNATIONAL AGRIBUSINESS
IN THE THIRD WORLD

Caesar Espiritu

In country after country in Asia and the rest of the
Third World, a growing phenomenon in the rural economy today
is transnational agribusiness. Rapid commercialization of
agriculture is going on in once-traditional societies.
Hitherto, rural communities concentrated their efforts on
production of food crops for subsistence and the local
market. Today, there are increasing activities related to
the processing and distribution of exportable farm products
and even the very manufacture of farm equipment.

The major actors in this new development have been:

a) transnational corporations;

b) Third World governments;

c) technologies; and

d) large landowners.

The primary instruments employed by such actors have
been new seeds, agricultural credit, agricultural inputs,
and farm equipment. Those mostly affected by such developments are the small farmers who find their farms diminishing
or being taken over through a proliferation of new technologies that changes their means of production. Although most

vitally affected, the small farmer has hardly any say in the decision-making processes which produce such "development." A new process of impoverishment has been initiated, and many members of the owner-cultivator-farmer community have become lessees, tenants, sharecroppers, or landless laborers, often working on the very land they used to own. Transnational agribusiness has also created a rise in the demand for seasonal labor and a growing class of migrant rural labor that finds itself being increasingly exploited.

The Commercialization of Agriculture

Rice, cassava, banana, coconut, beans, and a wide variety of vegetables have been the traditional subsistence crops of peasants and farmers in many developing societies. Fishing and poultry, swine, and cattle raising have also been familiar rural activities. The introduction of agribusiness, especially by transnational corporations (TNCs), has changed the lifestyles of peasants and farmers. Production methods have been modernized and mechanized. Intensified methods of cultivation to increase yields have been introduced. Less and less areas are being planted with traditional food crops. New commercial export crops are increasingly taking over lands, previously reserved for traditional subsistence crops. Moreover, corporate enterprises now influence the growing even of such traditional crops as rice, maize (corn), and bananas. Poultry farms and piggeries are being established, not by small farmers but by new corporate groups.

The most dramatic result has been a sharp change in social relationships in the farms, with large landowners increasing their landholdings and expanding through corporate farms into the operation of credit institutions and engagement in trading and marketing activities. With the appearance of corporate farming, the small farmers have become even more marginalized--in many cases, reduced to voiceless factors of production.

Conjunction of Interest of Government, Large Landowners, and TNCs

All of these developments have been induced and made possible by initiatives undertaken by governments and through their encouragement of efforts to increase agricultural production. In the wake of increasing populations, governments in developing societies have understandably spurred activities and projects to increase production, making productivity the barometer for measuring the success of government agricultural policies.

Lured by the promise of greater profits, transnational corporations have moved in with large capital and modern technologies to secure economies of scale. They are utilizing advanced marketing know-how, generally in alliance with big landowners and financiers whose hold on the rural economy has increased. Governments have encouraged this trend (and, in many cases, even supported it with government funding) in the belief that the commercialization of agriculture, including the introduction of new agricultural technologies, is the answer to the challenge of poverty in the rural areas and the need to feed the growing urban population. Moreover, where food crops can be replaced by agricultural exports, this would provide an effective means to earn scarce foreign exchange. In fact, many governments vie with one another in attracting to agriculture as much foreign investment as possible. Governments lacking popular support, and those which do not necessarily give priority to the needs of the poor, find transnational corporations natural allies in enhancing their goal of perpetuating themselves in power.

Local elites, for their part, have found the linkage with transnational corporations desirable and profitable. Big landowners, many of them absentee landlords in developing countries, have felt that there are insufficient economic rewards for traditional farm practices. Seeing the growing opportunities for profit in the export of agricultural products to the world market, they find it difficult not to yield to the initiatives of experienced global agribusiness companies in proposing economic alliances to modernize agriculture and in promoting an export-oriented strategy. Even nonagricultural corporate enterprises, seeing the growing stagnancy of industrial markets, have been joining TNCs in moving into what would appear to be the natural priority projects in developing societies, namely, the maximization of agricultural yields and the processing of the products of the soil. After all, natural resources constitute the chief and basic asset for most developing countries.

The Green Revolution and Rice Production

The production of rice, which is the staple food of more than two billion people, has indeed increased significantly with the introduction of agricultural technologies.

Doubtless, an agricultural breakthrough has been achieved
which, viewed in the aggregate, has the potential for increasing food security in this region of teeming populations. However, this has been achieved at the cost of the
traditional varieties which have been replaced by new varieties, some of which have proven to be more vulnerable to
pests. Moreover, the new varieties are dependent on expensive farm inputs--seeds, fertilizers, pesticides, and farm
machineries--which have exposed small farmers to completely
new needs for credit and to dependence on suppliers of
credit. The Green Revolution has thus entrapped many small
farmers in Asia into selling their landholdings or getting
deeper into debt, not only because the cost of farm inputs
are heavy but also because, in many instances, the increase
in rice prices have not kept up with the increase in cost of
production. To this should be added, in some countries
where land reform has been instituted (with much heraldry),
the cost of amortizing land taken from big landowners and
sold to the tillers.

The fact is that the technology of the Green Revolution
cannot really coexist with traditional systems of agriculture. In the case of India, the Green Revolution enhanced
the existing patterns of impoverishment and created new
opportunities for impoverishment. Small farmers, hitherto
able to meet their own traditional needs, now found themselves dependent because of the new technology and its
credit requirements. The net effects were: (1) impoverishment of the poor; (2) the strengthening of the power of
other more powerful groups, such as landowners whose domi-
nance was reflected in their effective blocking of such progressive legislation as agricultural income taxation; and

(3) the creation of agricultural systems which are energy-dependent. For example, 20 percent of export earnings in 1967 in India were used to pay the bill for fertilizer imports.

In Malaysia, the Green Revolution has had a negative impact on employment in that mechanization initially displaced labor. Even in Malaysia, where the program was run fairly well (with provision of government resources to make sure that small peasants have access to particular supports), the Green Revolution displaced small units of production with larger units of production. The reason is self-evident. The Malaysian government provided new seeds, agricultural machineries, irrigation, and fertilizer, but as an alternative to structural reforms of land ownership which the government did not want to undertake. The real crux of the problem of rural poverty in Malaysia lies in land ownership.

The technological breakthroughs of the Green Revolution have thus ended up exacerbating inequality in the rural areas. The avowed goal of many governments of modernizing agricultural production has, in fact, benefitted big farmers and impoverished the small ones.

In the meantime, successful linkages with the providers of modern technology and management, of fertilizers, pesticides, irrigation pumps, tractors, and power tillers have been forged by big landowners. The traditional rural economy if thus fast disappearing. Integration into the world economy is progressing virtually irreversibly.

The Hybridization of Maize Production

The modernization of agriculture has gone on not only with the Green Revolution in rice. In Africa, Mexico, the Caribbean, and in some areas of Asia, hybrid maize seeds are increasingly being grown, displacing many of the traditional staple varieties grown by farmers, such as the open-pollinated varieties. Brought in by TNCs, the new hybrid seeds are often propagated through arrangements with large local corporations, which have found agribusiness a most profitable complement to their industrial and financial activities. Without being subjected to the rigors of quality control testing, hybrid seeds which are directly imported are potentially subject to pest infestation. In the Philippines, with only three TNCs having oligopolyon hybrid maize seeds, two of the largest Philippine conglomerates have joined with them in producing the seeds in certain areas of Mindanao. These activities have been promoted by the government's classification of these agricultural activities as "pioneer" enterprises to encourage their production.

Soil Exhaustion

Agribusiness is spreading fast. Presented as an all-out effort to boost food production, governments, large landowners, industrialists, and TNCs have promoted agricultural modernization of all sorts. In the process, there has been much soil destruction and erosion caused by hasty decisions to create plantations that would cash in on rising demand among the industrialized countries.

In Mexico, for example, strawberry planters treat the soil carelessly in an effort to produce quickly. The application of too much irrigation and pesticide results in the soil being infested and exhausted. A study by Ernest Feder, *Strawberry Imperialism: An Enquiry into the Mechanisms of Dependency in Mexican Agriculture* (The Hague: Institute of Social Studies, 1977), documents how the strawberry millionaires merely count on taking over new land where the process can be started all over again. To compete with the greater "expertise" of U.S. procedures, the Mexican strawberry millionaires plunder resources to the fullest.

In the Philippines, the American TNCs (and their banana millionaire allies) have surrounded plantations with long ditches and canals, and have exhausted the richest lands in Mindanao in less than ten years of intensive banana production and exportation. Denudation of forests by Japanese trading companies with their Filipino logging associates have now caused continuous flooding in many places.

These practices are repeated in many developing countries. In some countries of Africa and Latin America, soil exhaustion and "desertification" have been going on at an alarming rate, giving rise to philosophical questions relating to the rights of succeeding generations over present natural resources.

Soil poisoning is one of the dire consequences of transnational agribusiness in developing countries. Chem-fertilizers--a necessary input in the production of high-yielding varieties of rice (as well as in the planting of such export crops as bananas) have initially induced boon harvests, but the plants have since become dependent on chemicals, fertilizers, pesticides, and modern irrigation. Moreover, after a while they actually reduce the capacity of the soil to produce because they have virtually destroyed the soil. Chemical residues, for example, have made lands, planted for five years to bananas, now barren in Davao.

Thus, transnational agribusiness has often left in its wake not only human impoverishment in the present-day context, but also massive degradation of the environment for production, raising the spectre of famine in the not too distant future. Transnational agribusiness has succeeded in most developing countries in not only mortgaging the present but also the future.

TRANSNATIONAL AGRIBUSINESS AND PLANTATION
AGRICULTURE: THE PHILIPPINE EXPERIENCE

Caesar Espiritu

Introduction

International demand has prompted many developing
countries to adopt agricultural policies emphasizing the
production of export crops. A prime actor in the implementation of such policies has usually been the transnational
corporation. The implementation of such policies has usually resulted in the displacement of smallholder farmers,
the displacement of land under food crop production for domestic consumption, and the adoption of agricultural technologies emphasizing economies of scale. The result has
been the creation of enormous plantations managed and controlled by powerful transnational corporations.

In country after country in Asia, the introduction of
large, transnational agribusiness plantations has left in its
wake the pauperization of erstwhile small farmers through
loss of land; hunger, indebtedness, and exploitation of most
of the laborers working on such plantations; and often permanent degradation of the physical environment on the plantation sites. The Philippines today provides one of the
most striking examples of the tragic long-term consequences
of the adoption of export-oriented agricultural policies
that virtually surrender sovereignty over large sections of

the rural economy to transnational agribusiness.

Expansion of Production of Commercial
Crops in the Philippines

Over the past decade and a half, the Philippine agricultural sector, dedicated to the production of export and luxury crops, animal feeds, and industrial raw materials, has expanded at a velocity which has completely eclipsed the considerably smaller increase of acreage and production of staple food crops.

The area devoted to production of food crops increased from 1960 to 1970 by 398.360 hectares, and from 1970 to 1980 by 1,811,250 hectares. The commerical crop area increased in the 1960s by 952,100 hectares, and during 1970 to 1980 by 1,365,800 hectares, for a total of over 2.3 million hectares. By the first half of the 1980s (for which we do not yet have comprehensive statistics), this area will have increased still more with the introduction of palm plantations on a large scale. And on the drawing boards are plans to convert sugar plantations into plantations of sorghum, yellow maize (corn), and soya beans. The real upsurge of the commercial sector occurred in the 1970s, with a particularly sharp increase beginning in 1973 with the advent of martial law government.

This general panorama does not fully reflect the unbalanced growth of the non-food sector. Some important food crops for domestic consumption are now really commercial crops, including certain fruits, vegetables, root crops for industrial purposes, and such animal feeds as maize. The portion of these crops, which is undoubtedly growing annually in both absolute and relative terms, is difficult to estimate. If only 15 percent of the area in "food crops" were shifted to "commercial crops," not available for immediate local consumption (being used for exports, animals, and the like), the two sectors would become about equal in size. Clearly, the sharp increases in a short period of time of most of the commodities cultivated in the country would not have been possible without the intervention of large plantation-type enterprises, even with respect to such staple foods as rice and maize.

All these factors have played an important role in the recent growth of agriculture in Mindanao, a favorite hunting ground of transnational agribusiness. The cropping area in Mindanao increased between 1970 and 1980 from about 2.9 million to about 4.7 million hectares, an increase of about 61 percent. This represents about 55 percent of the entire expansion of cropping in the country. Three commercial crops (coconuts, bananas, and pineapple) increased their hectarage by about 940,000 hectares, in contrast to the added 570,000 hectares in rice and maize. These increases were initiated by large-scale operators, including corporate farms and national and transnational agribusiness firms.

*Rural Development Strategies
and Rural Impoverishment in
the Philippines*

These significant shifts, which have taken place within a single decade in Philippine agricultural production, reflect a basic change in investment priorities away from "food crops" to high-value "commercial crops." This is in line with the new agricultural development strategies for the Third World devised by the industrialized countries--

strategies which have left massive rural impoverishment in their wake. These strategies have been heralded as ushering in a Green Revolution which was supposed to eradicate hunger and rural poverty in developing countries and make them nationally self-sufficient in their food needs. The actual results, of course, have been quite different.

The Green Revolution development strategy had been preceded by an earlier development strategy emphasizing land reform. The 1960s witnessed the Cuban revolution and, along with it, a program of land reform. The Cuban land reform sought to abolish the blatant inequities of pre-revolutionary Cuban agriculture and was expected to have a worldwide impact on peasant farmers. The United States, at first, endorsed so-called programs of land reform to forestall other socialist reforms in Latin America and elsewhere. For Latin America, the new strategy was formulated through the Alliance for Progress (1961) which proposed to make "land reforms" a prerequisite for financial assistance to Latin American governments.

The objective of such land reform programs was to increase agricultural output and productivity on the basis of slightly more equitable distribution of wealth and income, on the well-founded argument that the formidable inequities in the distribution of wealth and income were an obstacle to economic and social development. The land reform programs of the 1960s in Latin America (which reached the Philippines in the early 1970s) were clearly far from radical in their conception. Even so, they immediately were met by fierce opposition from the Latin American landed elites and from U.S.-based investors. Thus, in Latin America after only a very brief flurry with land reform, the Green Revolution

displaced land reform as the dominant development strategy.
This shift in development strategy soon reached the Philippines.

The Green Revolution strategy aimed at securing substantial increases in crop production through intensifica-
tion of cultivation and the employment of high-yielding
varieties of seeds, along with large inputs of chemical fertilizers and pesticides. The strategy, however, also resulted in fortifying the landed elites in developing countries economically, socially, and politically--as they were
the only ones able to afford these capital- and energy-
intensive inputs. As Ernest Feder points out in his *Rape of
the Peasantry,* the basic assumption of the Green Revolution
(even if usually unstated) was that large-scale food producers are more efficient than smallholders and that the new
technologies to bring about such a revolution could more
easily be transferred to them.

In the Philippines, the Green Revolution facilitated
the widespread entry of transnational agribusiness corporations engaged in the manufacture and distribution of the
fertilizers and pesticides necessary to grow high-yielding
varieties of rice. Such transnational agribusiness corporations undertook massive transfers of both capital and technology to the Philippines. The transfers occurred at all
levels of agricultural and agriculture-related activities,
from production to distribution (of both exports and imports),
and involved both outputs and inputs. Notwithstanding these
large investments, however, poverty, unemployment, hunger,
and malnutrition in rural and urban communities kept increasing. In fact, it became apparent that the greater the investments, the more explosive became these problems. A new

strategy--that of "assisting the poor"--was therefore inau-
gurated in the Philippines through World Bank-assisted
credit programs.

Assistance to the poor farmers was the avowed rationale
behind the massive Masagana 99 project to increase rice production in the Philippines in the mid-1970s. Prodded by
rural banks (which had to dispose of funds provided by the
World Bank), everyone in the rural areas of the Philippines
became farmers, since only farmers were entitled to the
bounty of the World Bank. It is well known, of course, that
in the end this nearly spelled out the collapse of the rural
banking system. The easy credit granted to genuine farmers
and "instant farmers" became difficult to recover. The initial increases in crop returns and the income thus generated
went to the purchase of luxury items, such as electronic
products and light trucks, rather than paying back the rural
banks. In the early years of Masagana, the defaults on re-
payments reached 90 percent.

Moreover, the World Bank's credit scheme could not
possibly be effective in rescuing the smallholders from their
abject poverty. This was precisely because no structural
changes in rural relationships were envisioned. And since
the major determinant of the direction and rate of change is
the existing inequality in distribution of wealth and power,
mere credit assistance and transfers could not induce much
development to rural societies. In the last three years,
yet another structure of production has been gaining cur-
rency, not only in the Philippines and Latin America but
throughout the developing world. It associates smallholders
(individually or in groups) and their modest resources with
large-scale farm operators, processors, and product buyers

(or at times, the government) through special contractual
arrangements. A typical arrangement is the production contract and outgrower scheme. The smallholders, using their
labor and the land they own or rent, turn over their output
to agribusiness in exchange for costly inputs under a loan
agreement accompanying the production contract. This production arrangement has been described as a nucleus estate
scheme.

In an excellent study (*Capitalism in Philippine Agriculture*), Rene Ofreneo records the expansion of the so-
called independent growers system or contract farming in the
Philippines to expand hectarage in banana, rubber, and rice
production, as well as in large commercial poultry and livestock firms. Two reasons for this expansion are the exhaustion of the agricultural land frontier and the distinct advantages for agribusiness firms in opting for such a system--
namely, production risks are passed on to the individual
growers; the danger of nationalization is precluded; and security from glut in the market is assured.

A variant of the production contract which is favored
even more by transnational agribusiness is the farm management contract. In the farm management contract, the land-
owner appoints a corporate executive or the firm itself as
manager or administrator of his land. The transnational
corporation thus essentially enjoys the same advantages as
if it had entered into a leasing contract.

A basic characteristic of modern transnational agribusiness is the high-geographic mobility of capital and technology which allows a corporation to relocate a new venture in
one country and abandon it in another (as in the case of the
Hawaiian pineapple plantations, transferred to the Philip-

pines and Thailand to take advantage of their low labor costs). An agribusiness corporation may completely pull up stakes in one country, or within a region in a country, and set itself up in another location for economic or political reasons without considering the social and economic impact on the original host country or region of such a move.

The relationship between transnational investment and the gargantuan debt now plaguing countries like Brazil, Mexico, Venezuela, and the Philippines has been made clear by Feder in *Rape of the Peasantry* and *Strawberry Imperialism*. Third world governments invite and accept foreign investments on the argument that they increase foreign exchange earnings. This is a highly questionable argument which does not clearly reveal the fact that local capitalists and some government officials reap benefits from their association with foreign investors. As foreign capitalists enter into overseas ventures, governments are obliged to subsidize the infrastructure and superstructure of a venture by means of loans from private sources or from bilateral and multilateral development assistance agencies. The servicing of these debts alone soon eats heavily into foreign exchange earnings and additional borrowings are needed in a never-ending vicious circle. Foreign investments not only create additional foreign exchange but exorbitant private and public debts. The United Nations, in fact, has noted that the countries that most attract the transnational corporations are also those that have borrowed most on the international capital markets.

Export-Oriented Agriculture and
Hunger in the Philippines

There are certain basic implications of the new and
varied structures of agribusiness described above. A study
by Francis Moore Lappe and Joseph Collins (*Food First: Be-*
yond the Myth of Scarcity) has pointed out that in Central
America and the Caribbean more than half the agricultural
land has been put into production for export. This export
push has been undertaken despite the fact that up to 70 percent of the children under five in many of the countries are
undernourished. During the winter and early spring, over
one-half of many vegetables in the American supermarkets now
come from Mexico. These vegetables have displaced beans, a
traditional food of the Mexicans. Similarly, the Brazilian
government has brought in Cargill and other giant U.S. grain-
marketing firms in an all-out drive to boost soya bean exports to the Japanese cattlefeed market, at the expense of
ordinary Brazilians whose basic food is black beans. In
Senegal, vegetables are flown by cargo jets every week to
European capitals. In Kenya, cut flowers and foliage are
grown under modern scientific methods for the ornamentation
of European homes and offices. Thus, competition has been
forged for scarce food supplies between a few well-fed people in Europe and North America, on the one hand, and the
mass of underfed people in Africa, Asia, and Latin America,
on the other.

In many other places, this same phenomenon is apparent.
The best Philippine and Taiwanese pineapples are destined
for U.S. and Western European markets. The best Philippine
tuna fish is shipped to the U.S. after it is processed in
Japan, where the lower-quality tunas are retained. Central

American bananas have long been going to U.S. and Western European markets. In recent years, the Philippines increased, by 50 times, the production of bananas for Japan. Production had decreased significantly by the end of the 1970s, with an increase in Japanese tariffs for bananas. However, Philippine exports of bananas to Japan are expected to rebound by 1985, with a decrease of Japanese tariffs (from 25 percent to 17 percent during the season, and from 17.5 percent to 15 percent during the off-season).

Indonesian, Malaysian, and Philippine forests are fast disappearing. Timber and lumber exports to Japan and the U.S. have denuded forest lands. Floods are now common in these countries as a result. All this switching of lands from traditional farm crops and the degradation of rain forest lands to increase export crop acreage are swelling poverty in the Philippines and, indeed, in most of the Third World.

Following the "Great Depression" in the Philippines in late 1983, a new policy has just recently been adopted to stop the growing of sugarcane in vast areas of Negros Island, where it has been grown extensively for the last 100 years, and to convert the lands into plantations of yellow maize, sorghum, and soya beans (whose international demand is supposed to be unlimited). In addition, by late 1984 huge tracts of land in Mindanao will be utilized for this new fad of the government in a crash program to halt the total collapse of the Philippine economy in the face of ever-worsening crises.

In the Philippines, crops for the international market occupy a heavy share of the funds and services of government agricultural programs to the neglect of local food crops.

Government funding has been generous for agricultural research which, in the end, benefits the agricultural TNCs.
Also, export expansion is the best incentive yet for local
elites to fight redistribution of agricultural resources.
In Malaysia, for example, government assistance for agricultural production has immeasurably increased as an alternative to structural reforms in land ownership. The number of
small farmers who have been transformed into landless
workers has hit an alarmingly high rate.

Today, however, the increased and ever-increasing costs
of inputs--fertilizers and chemicals--have wreaked havoc on
the small farmers in the Philippines, whose fields have been
prepared to grow high-yielding varieties of rice. These
fields can no longer easily revert to growing traditional
varieties, not requiring chemical fertilizers.

In the final analysis, the Philippine rural development
strategy has failed. The fundamental reason for this failure is the simple fact that the basic problem in the rural
areas is inequality in the distribution of wealth and power
and this problem was not meaningfully addressed. So long as
these conditions persist, great capital and technological
inputs will only aggrevate the phenomenon of domination and
exploitation on the farms in the Philippines.

Transnational Agribusiness
Plantations in the Philippines:
Some Case Studies

We have described above how the Green Revolution
strategy has ended up pauperizing Philippine small farmers.
Moreover, the Green Revolution brought with it a greatly expanded role for transnational agribusiness in the Philippines.

These transnational agribusiness corporations have introduced into Philippine agriculture modern plantations which
have become a major new source for rural exploitation and
impoverishment in the country.

(1) Banana Plantations in the Philippines

Perhaps the most striking case study of the impact of
international demand on domestic production and structures
of production is that of the banana industry in the Philippines. It highlights the concrete contradictions and limitations of attempted structural reforms of a neo-colonial
economy fully subordinated to and integrated with the world
capitalist market. The bulk of the Philippine transnational
corporation-dominated banana industry (about 80 to 90 percent) is located in Davao del Norte in Mindanao. There has
really been an explosion of banana production in the short
time span of about a decade--a development which is always
characterized by the chaos typical of rapid capitalist
expansion.

The first major shift toward new plantation crops for
export occurred in the mid-1960s with the lowering of tariff
for banana imports into Japan. The immediate result was
combined action by TNCs, government, and big landowners to
meet international demands by creating large banana plantations which have left in their wake immense socioeconomic
problems. The banana plantations are located in areas with
the widest expansion of irrigation facilities and with substantial access to rural electrification. The process of
establishing these large banana plantations has involved the
concentration of land ownership and a dramatic shift to production of bananas on land previously devoted to cultivation
of rice, maize, coconuts, coffee, abaca, and rubber. In the

process, there has occurred displacement of thousands of small landholders, peasants, tenants, and national tribal minorities from their land. There has also caused a rapid acceleration of the process of indebtedness of small farmers.

With the removal of Japanese restrictions on the importation of bananas in 1963, United Fruit Company and Standard Fruit Company, well known for their banana operations in Latin America, immediately sprang into action. The subsequent lowering of the tariff on bananas imported into Japan became so attractive that Del Monte, which had been producing pineapples in the country since the 1920s, decided to join the two other TNCs by branching out into banana production. From 1968 to 1975, the export earnings from bananas increased by 533 percent a year; in 1975 bananas had become the sixth largest export in the Philippines. By the second half of the 1970s, the export receipts from bananas exceeded $100 million a year, although it was only $1.35 million in 1969.

But Philippine bananas entered Japan in 1969 when there were already indications of over-importation from other sources. Nevertheless, Philippine banana exports grew in subsequent years, mainly because of lower prices. After 1975, demand began to sag in Japan. Philippine bananas may be said to have usurped the Japanese market at its last stage of dramatic growth, and apparently the type of banana exported from the Philippines did not command a premium any more. In other words, the extraordinary growth of Filipino production was the result of speculative actions on the part of global conglomerates. The costs of this speculation were borne primarily by Filipino producers and banana workers (and by Japanese distributors).

The overextension of plantations undoubtedly had an unbalancing effect on both large and small producers in the realm of prices paid or costs charged to producers--over and beyond the traditional sharp business practices of the fruit corporations. It must be assumed that as Philippine exports to Japan (and the Middle East) became fraught with difficulties in the late 1970s these corporate business practices became still sharper. The instability of the markets, the declining value of the real price of bananas, and the increasing costs of production intensified competition both among the transnational corporations in the industry and among the corporate growers (the large-scale, commercial banana producers, producing under contract for the corporations). These developments, in turn, had serious repercussions on small banana growers.

The Del Monte-Philippine Packing group obtained its bananas from 10 corporate farms, totaling over 6,000 hectares, through production and marketing contracts. Intensified competition in the late 1970s had worked to the immediate disadvantage of the less viable plantations. At least two plantations had either "phased out" their operations or were compelled to declare insolvency. In some cases, Del Monte was even provided with the opportunity to manage directly some of the depressed plantations. As a result, the corporate growers ended up with lesser bargaining strength vis-a-vis their TNC partners, although the corporate growers organized themselves to put pressure on Del Monte with respect to prices paid and costs of services provided under the Del Monte-grower agreements.

In contrast to Del Monte, the Dole-Stanfilco group operated its production extensively with about 375 small

growers, most of whom had been cajoled by Dole into abandoning rice, maize, and coconut cultivation with the promise of
fabulous financial benefits (which turned out, of course, to
be false for all except the larger smallholders). Like
other peasant farmers, their situation is characterized by
onerous debts which begin with the very transformation of
their small plots into banana production units. With the
financial "assistance" of the corporation, their debts grew
in the course of the years. Among the causes of indebtedness was an "anomalous pricing system," with prices being
dictated by Dole and not in conformity with the original
agreements. Quality and weight regulations (including re-
jects) and exorbitant input costs were charged against the
growers for plantation activities directly undertaken by the
corporation.

This was considered to be an ideal area because of its
soil fertility, accessibility, and topography. The company
signed a "joint venture" with a government agency, the Bureau of Prisons, to grow bananas and then sold the bananas to
United Fruit Company, whose subsidiary--the Mindanao Fruit
Company--provided the technical assistance. United Fruit
Company was thus shielded from attacks of "foreign control."
Apparently, the government was both willing and able to violate its own laws or change those which seem to be inconsistent with its thrust of encouraging foreign investments in
agriculture. Most of the lands now occupied by the banana
plantations in Mindanao were public agricultural lands,
whose acquisition and control are regulated by the public
land law and the Philippine Constitution.

The land acquisition scheme used local corporate
dummies to get around public land restrictions. The richest

lands were cleared by the labor or rehabilitated prisoners-- more than 850 hectares, growing tens of thousands of rubber, coconut, cacao, and coffee trees, as well as thousands of abaca plants. Here, as indeed in all of the banana planta- tions in the Philippines, it became apparent that the land- owners, especially the illiterate small owner-cultivators, were legally defenseless against powerful corporations.

The banana industry in the Philippines provides a classic example of how the interests of large landowners, TNCs, and government have, indeed, coincided. It was pre- determined from the start that concentration of land owner- ship was necessary to produce bananas efficiently. This was therefore accomplished through various arrangements, principally through lease and farm management contracts and with the amendment of certain laws of the Philippines to fa- cilitate such land acquisition schemes as the one described above.

(2) Pineapple Plantations in the Philippines

Del Monte is a giant agribusiness TNC which, although originally based entirely in the U.S., now operates in more than 24 countries. Its history in the Philippines is one of phenomenal growth with the unstinting support of the Philip- pine government. Its primary pineapple plantation has now been moved from Hawaii to the Philippines.

Castle and Cooke (whose products are known worldwide under the Dole label) is one of the 25 largest food corpora- tions in the U.S., and in 1979 ranked 210th among the For- tune-500 list of corporations. When Castle and Cooke shifted their main pineapple plantations from Hawaii to the Philip- pines (setting up a Philippine subsidiary DOLEFIL), they leased over 25,000 hectares of land in Mindanao. Most of the land was obtained with the assistance of the Philippine government. Much of the land is leased from the National Development Corporation (NDC), a Philippine governmental entity set up to authorize land purchased beyond the 1024-hectare constitutional limit and land rentals beyond the 2,252-hectare limit. Ironically, this land is excluded from the land reform program of the Philippines, a program which supposedly promotes the family farm as the base of Philippine agriculture!

According to local union leaders, Castle and Cooke's pineapple plantations in Mindanao claim twice the official land area of 25,000 hectares. They allege that much of the remaining area not leased from the NDC was in fact purchased from small farmers at depressed values. The company (DOLE-FIL), not surprisingly, denies that it owns any of its pineapple lands in Mindanao. Here, once again, NDC has played a crucial role. In the 1960s, following several years of drought, a Filipino businessman--Pedro Changco, Jr.--offered farmers in the area immediate cash payments for their farms. Many of the farmers were already in debt. Few has ever seen cash in the amounts offered ever in their lives all at one time. Several farmers accepted the offer and sold their farms. At the time, no one had any idea that the land was being bought for DOLEFIL operations. Since a foreign corporation could not own land in excess of a constitutionally prescribed limit, the NDC bought the land and leased it DOLEFIL.

An agreement between NDC and DOLEFIL reveals the nature of the relationship between the two. It provides that NDC shall--from time to time and when and as requested by Dole--buy, acquire, and obtain title to such additional parcels of land as may be needed by Dole in its operations under the agreement. In addition to the lands leased for its pineapple plantation, Dole has moved into large-scale rice production on 1,300 hectares in another province. Ironically, the impetus for this move has been provided by a Philippine law which requires that corporations with 500 or more employees must grow or purchase enough rice to feed their employees. Since the land reform act does not apply to these corporate rice farms, several large corporations are discovering that rice production can be a lucrative business too.

Dole claims that its workers receive higher than prevailing wages and a variety of fringe benefits. But the average, annual take-home pay amounted to ₱6,000 a year at a time when, according to Philippine government cost-of-living indices, the minimum needed for an average Filipino family is ₱12,775 a year. Moreover, the Philippines National Labor Relations Commission has found Dole in violation of local labor law and has ordered them to pay over $2 million in withheld harvest bonuses, factory-waiting time, and back wages due to workers fired in the late 1960s.

Castle and Cooke (DOLEFIL's parent corporation) has a policy of keeping its labor costs down by the use of seasonal and part-time workers, who account for the equivalent of 14,300 full-time workers in Castle and Cooke's worldwide work force of 40,000. Philippine law requires, however, that any casual worker employed for more than three months becomes a permanent employee, entitled to social security and other benefits from the employer. Castle and Cooke bypassed this law by using labor contractors who are paid by the corporation, a fee amounting to 20 percent of the labor costs of the labor supplied by the contractor. Thus, the workers are kept one step removed from the corporation and technically become temporary employees supplied through the chosen contractor. Moreover, the labor contractors regularly cheat their workers out of part of the wages due.

DOLEFIL has also shown little solicitude for the health of their workers. A list of chemicals used by DOLEFIL, drawn up by a company official in the Philippines, shows two carcinogenic pesticides banned from use in the U.S.--heptachlor and mirex.

The DOLEFIL plantation sites also display visible signs of soil erosion. The land used to be covered by trees and wild grass, with their root systems retaining water in the soil. As pineapples do not have a deep root system, the soil has drifted to the riverbed causing problems of silting. When the rains come, the riverbed overflows and floods the farmers' fields and even the towns.

(3) Oil Palm Plantations in the Philippines

The latest dramatic example of the development of a new export crop in the country is the recent government-initiated development of a palm oil industry in Mindanao. Palm oil provides about 15 percent of the vegetable oil traded on world markets. The crop is grown on plantations in Southeast Asia, Africa, and South America, and in numerous African smallholdings.

The National Development Corporation, the only entity empowered to own lands to excess of the constitutional limit of 1,024 hectares, was recently revitalized by the government, given additional powers, and its capitalization increased 22 times--from ₱450 million to ₱10 billion ($1.36 billion). Participating with the Philippine government in this development through the formation of joint ventures, are several Malaysian-based agribusiness TNCs under British and Malaysian control.   In Agusan del Sur and Surigao del Sur, following the issuance of Presidential Proclamation No. 1939 and 2041 in 1980, 40,550 hectares of land have been withdrawn from sale and set aside for plantation agriculture.

At the moment, there are six TNCs that have been set up to produce African palm oil at a total capitalization of ₱3 billion ($435 million) on 118,000 hectares of land.   Hundreds of thousands of settler farmers have been dislocated, including some whose families have lived on the land for two or three generations in the hope of acquiring title from the government.

Two of these plantations are joint ventures between the National Development Corporation and the Guthrie Corporation. Guthrie was originally a British transnational corporation with its headquarters in London.   It has since been purchased by the Malaysian government.   The first joint venture plantations of these groups covers a continuous 4,000 hectares, all of which have been planted to oil palms since mid-1981.   After Guthrie had entered into its joint venture with NDC, Dunlop entered into a similar agreement with NDC to develop another 8,000 hectares for palm oil plantations in the Agusan Valley, just south of the Guthrie plantation. However, due to considerable local opposition to the project, the causes of which NDC seemed unable or unwilling to rectify, they pulled out of the area in November 1981.

To acquire the land, the NDC-Guthrie Plantation, Inc. was first granted access to the site area by Presidential Decree No. 1939.   On April 8, 1980, NDC and Guthrie were incorporated to form NDC-Guthrie Plantations (NGPI), of which

NDC has 60 percent of the equity and Guthrie 40 percent. The agreement is that NDC purchases the land as its contribution to the partnership and makes it available to NGPI through an annual lease rental. In turn, Guthrie provides the technical expertise and assistance for a fee. In this way, Guthrie is able to get around the constitutional limit on foreign ownership of land over 1,024 hectares. NDC is entitled to dividends in the form of 1 percent of the net sales, and Guthrie in the form of 2 percent of the net profit.

The decree establishing NGPI reserves the land "for the use of NDC for agricultural plantation cultivation, subject to private rights, if any there be," but delimited the area without previously determining its current land-use patterns or occupation. Actually, several towns and village communities were included within the area, but NGPI nevertheless asked the residents to sign waivers. In return, residents either received a small sum for improvements or no payment by way of compensation (but a promise instead of employment on the plantation). The claims of ownership of those living within the site area were simply brushed aside. A number of fraudulent practices occurred, and as a result individual farmers have been transformed into agricultural laborers. Direct or indirect pressures were employed to induce the people to surrender their lands. Indeed, much of the low-land area suitable for annual crops has been appropriated by large plantations.

A second project of 4,000 hectares has been undertaken by the joint venture of the National Development Corporation and Guthrie, Inc., eventually to be known by a different name--the NDC-Guthrie Estates, Inc. (NGEI). This project

has been made possible with the grant of a loan of Ⱡ6.4
million by the British Commonwealth Department Corporation
(CDC) in January of 1983 as part of a tandem loan with the
International Finance Corporation (IFC). (The CDC is a
British governmental development agency set up to fund development projects through soft loans. The IFC is a member
of the World Bank group.)

Recently, many local people and grassroots groups
voiced complaints about the plantations, and ultimately
these came to the attention of the British Parliamentary
Human Rights Group. Two MP members of the Parliamentary
Human Rights Group (a quasi-official body) investigated, and
their report, *The CDC and Mindanao*--revealing a rather
shocking history of the project--in itself provides provocative reading for lawyers and others concerned with human
rights and alternative development.

This report and other evidence revealed that many
groups in the region concerned are unilaterally opposed to
"plantationizing" and "transnationalizing" their homelands.
Among their concerns are:

    a) plantations are, in effect, "expropriating"
        the lands of hundreds of small farmers--
        notably, tribal people living on ancestral
        lands;

    b) they are creating a new class of landless
        wage workers (allegedly underpaid) and now
        dependent on such foreign actors as Guthrie
        and NDC for their future economic security;

    c) the long-term future of palm oil production
        as a basis for "development" is bleak since
        chemical substitutes will soon displace
        already competitive markets for the product;

d) in any event, the major "profits" from the
enterprises are going to foreign investors
who have no long-term interest in Mindanao,
especially its people;

e) plantations are destroying valuable lands
used for food production necessary to
support local populations, and such mono-
culture will eventually destroy the productivity of the land as it is consumed by it;

f) the consortium has used unlawful means to
exercise lawless powers; and

g) the projects must be stopped because those
victimized presently have no basis for participating in the design, management, and
accountability of such development projects
(the present structuring of an enterprise
being such that no one need entertain, let
alone be held accountable to, the grievances of affected people).

The last issue concerning lack of participation takes
on even more color when the history of the project is revealed. In their report, the British MPs were shocked to
find that the plantations had condoned the use of criminal methods, even murder, to secure many of their present
estates. The managers had contracted with a para-military
force of ex-policemen (called the "Lost Command") to provide security against their allegedly hostile small farmer
neighbors. In turn, the Lost Command killed, tortured, or
intimidated many people who had protested to the plantation;
they systematically intimidated farmers to sell their lands
to "dummies" who in turn sold them at a profit to the companies. Further, the companies collaborated in a "nominee"
system of employment: by contract it empowered various local
figures to "nominate" others to become plantation workers--a
process which in turn enabled the nominators to demand a

share of the nominees' wages. The companies had refused to recognize the workers' union claims, and the Lost Command exterminated union and other organizers. These were some of the findings of the MPs after several weeks' investigation in Mindanao. Their remedy? A stern admonition to CDC to do something to prevent such "grave errors in judgment" in the future, and to urge the plantation companies to live in greater harmony with their "host" communities and their workers!

Philippine Rural Development Policies: Whose Development?

The case studies presented above indicates that basic trends in the rural areas do not augur well for small farmers and peasants. A growing literature on development stresses the need for far-reaching internal structural transformation in the developing countries to ensure the development of peoples. But the present tide seems to run against the establishment of such far-reaching internal changes. On the contrary, the existing exploitative social, political, and economic structures have been given free rein and even strengthened in the name of "development."

Agriculture in the Philippines has fast become capitalistic. The trends are such that at the turn of the century, one may no longer be able to envision purely agrarian communities of small farmers and peasants with their draft animals. Internal, integrated agricultural operations shall have taken place, involving the whole agricultural chain from different structures of production to production inputs, food processing, management, the supply of credit, leadership, and even government relations. Subsistence farming, the products

of which do not enter the monetized economy, shall have
disappeared. Success in modern agriculture will inevitably
require intensive capital.

A corollary to this is the growth of corporatism in
agriculture. If agricultural activities must be integrated,
if technologies must be introduced, if capital formation becomes imperative as the agricultural process becomes more
and more specialized and complex, then agricultural corporations have to be organized. Agribusiness departments or
subsidiaries of existing industrial corporate firms have to
be constituted. In fact, even now these trends are evident
all over the developed world. No doubt, the entry into
agriculture of both local and transnational corporations is
inevitable, given present Philippine policies on agriculture.

In many places, the transition into predominantly capitalist structures and the growth of corporations in the
farms has meant land concentration and centralization. One
now sees a countermovement to the land reforms of a generation or two ago. With growing mechanization comes a need
for economies of scale. The enclosure movement in England
two centuries ago is not without its current versions in
such developing countries as the Philippines.

The twin linchpins of Philippine agricultural policies
have been the adoption of "modern" high-yield varieties
(HYV) and seed technology and the development of export-
oriented, large, "modern" agribusiness plantations. Both
policies have exacerbated hunger and impoverishment in rural
areas of the Philippines.

Hungry mouths are increasing, even in the rice bowls of
Central Luzon in the Philippines where rural incomes have
decreased substantially--not in spite of, but because of,

the high-yielding varieties of rice to which these areas
have been planted over the last ten years. The cost of pesticides and fertilizers needed to grow these varieties has
risen far beyond the means of the farmers, and the credit
system has doomed them to eternal debt to the rural banking
system. Meanwhile, the deadly chemicals of transnational
fertilizer companies have killed the snails and fish in rice
farms, formerly an important source of protein for small
farmers. In their anguish, the farmers try to return to the
traditional varieties that at least gave them subsistence,
but they have sadly discovered that they can barely undertake even this anymore since most of the plant varieties
have been displaced by high-yielding varieties.

And the arithmetic of exploitation is rising to geo-
metrical proportions in Central Luzon. Not only have subsistence farmers been removed from their traditional lands
because of a hydroelectric project; now, the waters of the
dam, already at low level, are being diverted toward the
lands of the powerful!

In Nueva Ecija, traditionally the premier rice-growing
province of the Philippines, less than 3 percent of the prospective beneficiaries of land reform have been able to pay
the amortization of their farms precisely because of their
increased pauperization. So at the end of the amortization
period of 15 years (in 1987) who will own these farms? Re-
leasing tenants from the bondage of the soil has been the
pompous slogan of the government for land reform. Now the
grim prospect is that peasants will become landless workers
in 1987!

Plantations, on the other hand, are by their very
nature a form of agricultural development which reduces un-

acceptably the level of participation of local communities
in their own development, and tends to transform independent
farmers into agricultural laborers. The Philippine experi-
ments with agribusiness plantations has brought about pauperization, hunger, dependency, and exploitation, not only
for its rural people but for the Philippines as a nation as
well. This raises the basic question of whose development
the Philippine government has really been interested in when
they initiated and encouraged the modernization and transnationalization of agriculture? One immediately realizes
that the development efforts in the Philippines (and indeed
in many developing countries) has not really been directed
at meeting the basic needs of people for food, clothing, and
housing. On the contrary, agribusiness is now fundamentally
oriented to exports. This creates a situation where the
well-fed few in the First World compete with the underfed
many of the Third World for land in the latter's own countries on which food crops can otherwise be grown to alleviate starvation.

The peoples of the Third World, thereby, not only become vulnerable to external shocks--to the vicissitudes of
demand and price fluctuation in the world market. They also
are not assured the food security they are entitled to for
survival (much less existence under conditions in which
their lives are made more human) under these acute stresses
of economic growth.

References

Alf Dubs and Colin Moynihan, *The CDC and Mindanao* (Report for the Parliamentary Human Rights Group), United Kingdom: Parliamentary Human Rights Group, 1983.

Ernest Feder, *Rape of the Peasantry*, New York: Anchor Books, 1971.

_____, *Strawberry Imperialism: An Enquiry into the Mechanisms of Dependency in Mexican Agriculture*, The Hague: Institute of Social Studies, 1977.

Dorothy Freisen and Gene Stoltzfus, *Castle and Cooke in Mindanao* (Discussion Paper No. 5), Third World Studies Center, University of the Philippines, January 1978.

Francis Moore Lappe and Joseph Collins, *Food First: Beyond the Myth of Scarcity*, Boston: Houghton Mifflin Company, 1977.

Rene Ofreneo, *Capitalism in Philippine Agriculture*, Quezon City: Foundation for Nationalist Studies, 1980.

Third World Studies Center, "TNC Control of the Philippine Banana Industry" in *AMPO Japan-Asia Quarterly Review*, Vol. 13, No. 3, 1981.

PROCESSING, PACKAGING, PROMOTION (PPP):
POLITICAL ECONOMY OF FOOD MODERNIZATION

Reginald Green

Processing, packaging, and promotion are the distinctive elements that make up modern food systems. Such modern systems are markedly different from traditional peasant and pre-modernized capitalist systems. The differences are primarily downstream from the farm--although they often feed back farm production and reinforce trends toward modernization of inputs and production practices.

In contrast with pre-modernized food systems, the processing, packaging, and promotion (PPP) of food results in a branded, highly advertised processed product. As an example, milk--previously bottled fresh at the milking site or close to it and promoted minimally (if at all) in the immediately surrounding area--under modernized food systems may be condensed and canned, have a brand name (e.g., Nestle), be highly advertised, and sold not only in more affluent rural areas but also throughout a country's urban areas. Thus, while the processing and canning plant in the above example may be located near the dairies involved in the milk production, it is often far from the retail outlets which sell the final product; indeed, many of these may be outside of the country.

The Logic of Modernization

For a *capitalist firm* modernization is logical because processing and packaging, backed by promotion, allow for wider profit margins than can be obtained on most unprocessed or semi-processed goods. Through modernization larger quantities can also be marketed over a broader area, resulting in resource-saving from technical economies of scale, as well as oligopolistic economies of scale by limiting the number of potential competitors to those with substantial capital and knowledge bases.

From the *technological* point of view, processing and packaging (and promotion if one includes soft technologies) also have physical attractions. They reduce physical loss-- or at any rate loss beyond the producer. PPP systems often have very high rejection/destruction rates in respect to crops offered for purchase. They foster mass production and make possible the creation of new products (and their identification to the consumer).

Consumer logic also favors modernization, at least up to a point. Modernization allows for provision of a greater variety of foods, more stably over the year, with more predictability of quality (at least by eliminating totally unsatisfactory products), and in forms requiring less preparation time and/or affording greater portability (e.g., a package of sliced bread requires less preparation time than a mixture of flour-yeast-water-salt, and a package of porridge is more portable than cassava).

Agents of Change

Food system modernization is spearheaded by medium-to-large-sized firms either at the processing/packaging or the wholesaling/retailing stage (*rarely* are such firms active in actual primary food or input production). These may or may not be transnational corporations (TNCs). There is some evidence from Central American studies that the initial stages are usually carried out by local firms, using imported machinery and methods, which are later bought up by TNCs when their markets are large enough to be attractive parts of a global empire.

At several levels it makes little difference whether TNCs or domestic firms are dominant. The effects discussed below on consumers and producers will vary little. However, at the national level, TNCs will tend to "export" a higher proportion of surplus (as dividends, trademark fees, technology charges, tied sales of inputs, overcharging, etc.) and may have a tendency to import more and buy/process less locally. Therefore, their impact on national production and balance of payments transactions may be worse than is the case with domestic firms.

PPP and the Consumer

The positive impact of food modernization on the consumer has been noted above. However, there are less desirable results.

First, processing, packaging, and promotion usually *raise the cost per calorie* substantially more than economies of scale and distribution reduce it. Condensed milk costs more per unit than fresh milk, potato chips than potatoes, or tomato paste than tomatoes.

Some parts of modernization, such as supermarkets, do reduce cost to the consumer, especially in high-wage economies. However, the overall impact is still normally cost-raising, even in the North, and much more so in low-wage Southern economies.

Second, many modern foods are of rather *dubious nutritional value*, both absolutely and (even more) relative to other foods which they tend to squeeze out of consumer diets. The most evident absolute example is Coca Cola. Taken as a group, "fast foods" may have the greatest negative nutritional impact on shifting diets.

Third, at least as promoted and used under Third World conditions, some modern foods constitute *serious dangers to health and life*. The most notorious examples are currently in the infant formula and baby food cluster of products.

PPP and the Poor Consumer

Modernized food systems, to the extent they do impinge significantly on eating habits, have a particularly negative impact on the poor consumer. First, he cannot afford to substitute higher cost, labor-saving (i.e., pre-processed) foods because to do so reduces total nutrient value available. Second, because the total food budgets of poor households are limited, shifts to convenience foods almost inevitably change (and worsen from a nutritional point of view) the makeup of the food basket. As men are most likely to buy and eat convenience and fast foods, they may also reduce significantly the food available to their wives and children.

These two considerations interlock with the *demonstration effect*, backed by promotion. This does not necessarily relate to true characteristics of the product. Guiness is sold as "good for you" or for "power" (admittedly probably truer than for most patent medicines); Coca Cola and its brethren are somehow associated with status; infant formulas (often quite falsely) as the way to give an infant a good start in life. The man who drinks Guiness to be strong or who buys Coca Cola to assert his worth or responds to his wife's plea to buy infant formulas for their child is almost always jeopardizing his family's nutritional standards and sometimes his baby's life.

The general impact of food modernization on diets of the rural poor of the South and on urban poor outside Latin America and the Caribbean can easily be overstated. However, at least in Asian cities it is growing. Even today for three or four production groups--Coca Cola and its brethren, infant formulas, tomato paste, and tinned fish-- there is substantial penetration, the results of which are, on balance, unambiguously bad in the first two cases and open to grave doubt in the latter two. Infant formulas *are* suitable for some cases under specified conditions which suggests distribution via the medical system, not that of high-powered hucksterism. Tomato paste is very timesaving, at a cost. Tinned fish may be cheaper but has a very negative effect on local small-scale producers.

Impact on Poor Producers

For the most part, the key actors in modernizing food processes buy their raw materials. There are exceptions (bananas and tinned fish) but, in general, processing, packaging, and promotion (including distribution) are more profitable than the actual growing. Even plantation systems in many cases (e.g., Philippine bananas) are being transformed into rural "putting out" systems with peasants tied to an interlocking package of technology, debt, and input supplies, who are formally (but not practically) independent business proprietors, replacing direct-hire labor on large, centrally handled units.

From the small producer's point of view the main dangers are:

a) he may be squeezed off his land because a medium-sized farmer is more able to meet the PPP buyer's requirements for scale and certainty of delivery;

b) or, if he does get a one-crop/one-buyer contract, he may in fact (by long-term contract, by debt, and/or by loss of land quality under intensive mono-cropping) lose his freedom to alter crop patterns and selection of buyers more or less permanently, and, in extreme cases, lose the opportunity to grow his own food (if his buyer feels such use of land is ineffi-cient to him, for example, by raising risk of diseased or blemished crops);

c) by *de facto* tying, the degree of exploi-tation of the peasant may be increased and his absolute net income reduced (as seems to have happened in respect to banana farmers in the Philippines); and

d) the PPP axis may reduce markets for some products, such as fresh fish, lo-cally produced tomato paste, or staple foods "downgraded" by white bread and potato chips. These are often produced by particularly low-income fishermen and peasants.

Particular problems arise in respect to crops with sharp seasonal demand or supply patterns. Unless these co-incide, small producers will find that they are forced to sell all of their output at a set (low) price during the short (high price on traditional markets) season, but may not be guaranteed purchases of all output during the high

(low price or none on alternative markets) season when it
is supply that varies. When demand is seasonal PPP buyers
will often enforce the right to alter offtake in ways which
require the peasant to maintain (and buy inputs for) excess
capacity.

Legal Resources and Food System Modernization

Food system modernization as such is not necessarily an
evil to be resisted. However, its negative impacts on specific groups of poor people, in particular places and at
given times, are at issue.

Legal resources can be of value in supporting education
and mobilization of those adversely affected, and in devising frameworks of enforceable controls. Of course, legal
controls (and a *fortiori* their enforcement) cannot be set in
place purely or even primarily by the actions of lawyers.
They must be the product of demands by adversely affected
consumers and producers.

Education includes making known the bad effects of the
modernization system; the legal limitations which exist on
paper and how they might be used in practice; and what might
be done by direct action, by political pressure, and/or by
securing new legal frameworks. Legal resources must be
developed through efforts to describe the existing legal
framework, show its potential uses, and demonstrate how it
might be strengthened. Less evidently, they include advice
on how to avoid libel and slander--TNCs are often litigious,
and people's organizations can ill afford the costs of these
kinds of cases.

Mobilization flows from education and consciousness-
raising. Legal resources to aid mobilization may include

advice on how to implement law-oriented targets. In addition, many producer and consumer bodies do have uses for "internal constitutional law," i.e., organizational, administrative, decision-taking, and dispute resolution procedures--areas in which legally trained people can make contributions if they are willing to venture outside formalism and engage in innovative adaptation.

Legal action and lobbying includes taking cases to officials or courts or making clear such action will follow unless a resolution of grievances is negotiated sooner. Both are areas in which legally trained persons, acting in support of consumer and producer bodies, have something to offer. Lobbying for new legislation or regulations is a related activity.

It should not be assumed too readily that existing or attainable laws and their enforcement have nothing to offer. Campaigns to limit operations of the TNC trawlers in traditional inshore fishing areas. ending abusive "middlemen/toil collector" exactions, creating regulatory frameworks against infant formula promotion, and limiting the use of some foreign trademarks/brand names (e.g., Coke in India) have proven possible in a fairly wide range of contexts. To date, this is not an area in which TNCs or their allies in the South have seen local mobilization and local action to be so dangerous that they must be stamped out on sight, or concessions on particular cases to be so generally damaging that they must be fought tooth and nail. Therefore, situations in which legal resources may be of significant use in ways similar to more standard client education--advice, negotiating support, and legal action--are still likely to be fairly common.

III. SOCIAL IMPACTS OF NEW TECHNOLOGIES
      ON THIRD WORLD AGRICULTURE

REAPING THE WHIRLWIND: SOME THIRD WORLD
PERSPECTIVES ON THE GREEN REVOLUTION
AND THE "SEED REVOLUTION"

Clarence Dias

The Green Revolution: High-Yielding
Varieties (HYVs) Yield High and
Varied Rural Impoverishment

One of the more obvious, and yet more painful lessons
learned from the Green Revolution is that the impact of technologies is powerfully influenced by contemporary social,
political, and economic relationships.

During the 1960s, amidst much publicity that a solution
for the world food crisis was near at hand, the HYVs were
pioneered in Mexico (at CIMMYT, the International Maize and
Wheat Improvement Center) and then introduced into India and
Pakistan and the Philippines (in the latter case, primarily
through IRRI, the International Rice Research Institute). The
HYVs represented a pure technical solution through which
hunger, it was hoped, would soon be a thing of the past. Increased food production (made possible by the HYVs) would ensure that there would be enough food for all. In 1970, the
"father" of the Green Revolution, Dr. Norman Borlaugh, won
the Nobel Peace Prize.

In the mid-1960s, the first IRRI-perfected HYBV not only
doubled but tripled traditional crop harvests. Soon after,
five major new varieties of HYVs were discovered and made

public so that there were appropriate HYVs for practically
all kinds of soil and weather conditions for rice cultivation. Asia's Green Revolution had been launched by IRRI's
achievements. For Latin America, CIMMYT's initial achievements were also spectacular. Mexico soon turned from being
a maize-importing to a maize-exporting country. Today,
CIMMYT wheat grows on over 30 million acres around the globe.
In the Philippines, by 1971-72 about 63 percent of the low-
land rice areas were planted to IRRI HYVs. Thanks to HYVs,
Mexican wheat yields have leaped from 12 to 50 wheat bushels
per acre, and by 1972-73 HYVs were contributing a billion
dollars a year to Asian cereal harvests.

But these successes were not all they seemed to be.
Today, Mexico imports both wheat and maize (or corn) again
from the U.S. The negative effects of the Green Revolution
on poor rural people have been so numerous that Ernest Feder
was prompted to assert that "the green revolution wreaks
havoc on underdeveloped countries."[1] A brief description of
India's experience with the Green Revolution will help identify some of the more poignant lessons to be learned from a
revolution that sought to eradicate hunger but ended up perpetuating rural impoverishment.

In the mid-1960s, in India (and probably in the Philippines too), HYVs were introduced through a propaganda bar-
rage conducted by the government. A great amount of government subsidy went to the early propagation and marketing of
HYVs and the required fertilizer inputs. Cultivating these
new seeds required considerable departure from the typical
prevailing practices of traditional subsistence or near-
subsistence agriculture.

Traditionally, an Indian peasant family would plant

seed saved from his own previous crop, use a fertilizer manure supplied by his own animals, and retain a major part of the crop produced for family consumption. They would be dependent only marginally on the market and usually, such cash as they required would be obtained by part-time work for wages, and sale of vegetable products, milk, chickens, etc. A complex system of inter-family or clan supports provided insurance against individual crop failures or other disasters.

Not only is such a traditional system of farming inappropriate for cultivating HYVs, but the Green Revolution has required the deliberate and systematic dismantling (under the euphemism of "modernizing" agriculture) of such traditional systems. Early in the Green Revolution, Arthur Moser (the then President of the Agricultural Development Council) argued that the cooperative social structure evident in many agrarian communities needed to be dismantled in order to encourage "aggressive interest in the marketplace."[2] The assumption of the HYV architects was that the Third World needed only to duplicate the farming practices of the First World to achieve food self-sufficiency. Within the space of two decades, the varied agricultural systems of the Third World and their surrounding social structures have been uprooted, overthrown, and replaced by a new Western model.

For the poor peasant, cultivating the new varieties of HYVs exposed him to new uncertainties and new opportunities for being exploited and dominated. The hybrid seeds must be bought at the beginning of each season. Moreover, as became apparent very early, the potential yields of HYVs are only realizable through the increased use of chemical fertilizers. In turn, the use of fertilizers intensified the incidence of weeds. Together with the fact that HYVs are more vulnerable to pests and diseases, this meant that in order to have a high-yielding harvest, larger amounts of fertilizer, irrigation, and pesticides were needed than with traditional varieties bred for tolerance to environmental stress and not just for high yields with high inputs. These inputs had to be available when needed. This, in turn, meant that for a poor peasant, enough of his previous year's crop had to be sold at a sufficiently high price to cover his costs. Even where this was possible, subsistence and other expenditures rarely left the peasant with the working capital needed at the start of each crop year, creating a vicious circle of dependence on credit for purchases. Interest charges often wiped out much of what would be recovered by way of eventual sale of the surplus crop.

Moreover, high vulnerability to pest and disease attacks on the new varieties often meant that even after expensive outlays, the peasant farmer found himself facing loss of a large part of his crop. Some small landowners have lost their land by getting into debt while attempting to grow HYVs. As the value of land to those able to afford the cultivation of the new varieties of HYVs increased, tenants and small landowners were forced off their lands by various legal and illegal means, thus causing an increase in the number of landless laborers.

Simultaneously with this pauperization process, the Green Revolution in India also brought with it a process of perpetuating dependencies. Peasants do not have access to the resources necessary to grow HYVs successfully. Attempts by the Indian government to provide these resources have consistently failed because the distributing agencies have been dominated by the richer and more powerful families in the community who succeeded in diverting the benefits of government programs to themselves. The economic power of the larger landowners increased as the poorer peasants grew more impoverished and became trapped in debt transactions which made it increasingly difficult for poor farmers to escape from their poverty. The success of the already richer farmers in cultivating HYVs led to an inevitable increase in their wealth, influence, and ability to control the land.

The rich not only increased the size of their land-holdings but also increased their share of benefits from the distribution of inputs and infrastructure essential for "modern" agriculture, such as tubewells and tractors. Increased mechanization exacerbated rural unemployment and underemployment, setting in motion the drift towards the cities. A World Bank study estimates that for each tractor purchased in Pakistan, between 7.5 and 11.8 full-time jobs are lost. After the purchase of a tractor the average farm size increased by 240 percent within three years, mostly through the eviction of tenants. Employment per cultivated acre dropped by 40 percent.

Many of these inequitable impacts were not entirely unintentional since the target farm group in the Green Revolution was typically the middle-class farmer. As a Ford Foundation document expressed it at the time, "only middle-class farmers could take the risk involved and would show the creativity to respond to the new technology."[3] "Risk" was an appropriate word. A farmers' cooperative in the Philippines recently complained that IRRI seed which had yielded as much as 8 tons per hectare at test plots was

yielding only 1.75 tons in the farmers' fields. This yield
was lower than some traditional varieties with more disease
resistance and less need for commercial fertilizers and
other dangerous chemicals. Given ideal conditions and large
amounts of fertilizers and chemicals, Green Revolution seeds
will respond well and provide high yields. However, if any
of the required inputs do not arrive on time, or are absent
altogether, farmers may experience extensive and expensive
crop failures.

The Green Revolution has adversely affected small landowners in other ways, contributing both to their impoverishment and to their malnutrition. Most small landowners traditionally practice a multi-cropping system, e.g., a mixture
of corn (or maize) and beans. Some experts have calculated
that companion-planting can increase both yield and profitability by more than 50 percent. Moreover, companion-planting makes a major contribution to the protein consumption of
subsistence farmers and their families. The new HYVs of
corn do not grow well together with other legumes. Half the
Third World's protein comes from food legumes. These legumes are being displaced both because of inability to companion-planting and also because of pressure on cultivable
land. Thus, for example, per capita legume production in
India dropped by 38 percent between 1961 and 1972 because
grain varieties were highly subsidized, making legumes less
attractive and less profitable.

The above survey of some of the impacts of the Green
Revolution makes it clear that the Revolution has done little
to aid the poor. Estimates in Indonesia indicate that no
more than 25 percent of peasant farmers benefited in any way
from the Green Revolution. The middle-class farmers, the

rich landowners (and, as will be demonstrated later, transnationals) have been the principal beneficiaries of the
Green Revolution. But for the impoverished masses in rural
areas the Green Revolution fostered pauperization and dependency. The kind of rural development resulting from the
adoption of the technology of the Green Revolution has resulted in increased urbanization as the poor were driven
from their fields and forced into a life of squalor in the
cities where they were faced with the cruel irony of having
to buy expensive cereals grown in fields where they once
harvested inexpensive legumes.

Development policies and programs are sometimes justified on the ground that even if they do cause hardships for
the poor in the short run, they will lead to the benefit of
the entire nation (including the poor) in the long run. In
the next section, we evaluate some of the impacts of the
Green Revolution at the national level in developing
countries.

The Green Revolution: Toward
National Pauperization

The Green Revolution was the means through which
developing country governments would alleviate the hunger
and poverty of their people. It has instead contributed to
the impoverishment of these countries in a variety of ways.

A few examples will help to assess the contribution
made by the Green Revolution to alleviating hunger:

-- in 1973-74, farmers in Bengal lost 80 percent of their rice crop (plus seedlings for
   the next crop) when they planted--according
   to instructions--new semi-dwarf rice in the
   river delta. High water destroyed the crop

where the old varieties might have survived;

-- in 1975, Indonesian farmers lost a half
   million acres of rice to leafhopper insects;
   and

-- in 1972, Brazil lost half its crop of wheat
   when it was attacked by a non-Mexican disease it was not bred to withstand.

Perhaps the most telling example is provided by Norman
Myers:

> A few years ago, one of the prized developments
> of the Green Revolution, a strain of rice known
> as IR-8, was hit by Tungro disease in the Phil-
> ippines. When rice growers switched to another
> form, IR-20, this hybrid soon proved badly vul-
> nerable to grassy stunt virus and brown hopper
> insects. So farmers moved on to IR-26, a super-
> hybrid that turned out to be exceptionally re-
> sistant to almost all Philippine diseases and
> insect pests. But it proved too fragile to the
> islands' strong winds, whereupon plant breeders
> decided to try an original Taiwan strain that
> had shown an unusual capacity to stand up to
> winds--only to find that it had been all but
> eliminated by Taiwan farmers who by then had
> planted virtually all rice lands with IR-8.[4]

These examples are not stray incidents based on individual instances of things going wrong. They are rather the
consequences of Green Revolution technology. To a large extent *genetic erosion* is a result of the Green Revolution as
the Philippine example so graphically illustrates. As old
varieties disappear, and as genetic uniformity spreads in the
Third World, we will witness an increasing incidence of dev-
astating crop disasters. The extensive use of chemical herbicides and pesticides hastens the process of pest mutation.
In Pakistan, for example, angry rice farmers joke that the
"miracle rice has led to miracle locusts."

Much of the increased yield surrounding use of HYVs is due to the heavy application of fertilizers and herbicides, many of which are petro-chemical based. As one World Bank staffer puts it, "between 75 and 90 billion pounds of Asian rice are directly dependent upon Middle East petroleum." By 1967 India was already paying out 20 percent of its export earnings on fertilizers. When cheap energy vanished in the 1970s, the Third World found itself saddled with an energy-dependent agricultural system. Fertilizer shortages in 1974 resulted in a loss of 15 million tons of grain--enough to feed 90 million people. Ninety-seven percent of the world's pesticides come from the industrialized countries, but thanks to the Green Revolution, Third World consumption is up to 20 percent and rising. Third World countries are increasingly finding that serious environmental problems are being imported along with their imports of fertilizers, herbicides, and pesticides and at an ever-escalating cost in foreign exchange at that! The price of the seed itself has more than doubled since the early days of the Green Revolution.

Pat Mooney identifies those whom the Green Revolution has benefited most:

> The Green Revolution has been undeniably profitable for agribusiness. By the sixties, agricultural enterprises were in need of a new market to maintain their growth. Bilateral and multilateral aid programs made expansion into the Third World financially possible. Twenty years later, major agrichemical firms have achieved a worldwide distribution system able to market successfully in Asia, Africa and Latin America. The Green Revolution was the vehicle that made all this possible.[5]

Under the pretext of feeding the hungry, the Green Revolution has ended up dragging into the Western market economy both the crops and the farming systems of Asia, Africa, and Latin America.

Toward a Green Counter-Revolution

Proponents of the Green Revolution are claiming that it has now entered a second phase: many of the criticisms have been accepted. As a Rockefeller Foundation official put it, "the critics have turned us around." Thus, some Green Revolution scientists are increasingly looking to local crops (vegetable and fruit) and the emphasis is changing from "breeding for yield to breeding for hardiness." But many in the Third World wonder whether it is not too late to turn the Revolution around. In 1978, *The Wall Street Street Journal* asserted in a front page article, "There isn't anything left in the Green Revolution's bag of tricks. The Revolution, in fact, has turned against itself."[6]

However, from a Third World point of view it might be dangerous to accept either of the above perspectives. What is probably needed is nothing less than a counter-revolution based upon an understanding of how the Green Revolution itself was used to create and reinforce structures of impoverishment.

There is nothing intrinsically wrong with the idea of increasing crop yields. But pure technological solutions are seldom "pure." Technology is not neutral. Most natural scientists tend to dismiss as "peoples' problems" or "social and cultural constraints" what happens to the technology they have actually developed once it is being utilized by real-life people. However, the purpose of science and technology must be to benefit people; and this purpose must determine the form that the scientific effort takes and the criteria by which it must be judged. Natural scientists must forsake neutrality for a value system which includes a practical concern for human life and welfare and the equitable distribution of resources and services.

The Green Revolution technology is biased in some much more blatant ways. It is perhaps true to say that from its very inception it has been biased against the poor who cannot afford to pay for the seeds, fertilizers, pesticides, irrigation, and equipment. However, it would be straining credibility to accept this bias as being inadvertent. The 1960s witnessed excess supply in the transnational fertilizer industry. This meant, from the perspective of the industry, that new markets were essential.

Not surprisingly, the HYVs owe their high yield to high inputs of chemical fertilizers. The potential for actually increasing chemical consumption is great since through seed coating and pelleting it becomes possible to utilize the seed "as a delivery system for chemicals and biologicals to the field." Lester Brown, in 1967, was optimistic that, thanks to the Green Revolution, the U.S. would be able to increase its fertilizer exports from U.S. $1 billion per annum to U.S. $7 billion. All that was necessary to accomplish this was to raise Third World demand for fertilizers to one-quarter of the per acre application of Japanese farmers. Bilateral and multilateral aid programs did their bit to help achieve this objective. During the sixties, transnational agribusiness was in need of new markets to maintain their growth. Thanks to the Green Revolution there was, in the words of the *U.S. News and World Report,* "an

increased demand for U.S. farm tools, fertilizers, pesticides, irrigation pumps and other agricultural equipment."[7]

Another example of technological bias resulting from
the influence of agribusiness can be found within the seed
itself. HYVs of many crops are "hybrids," i.e., the offspring of two distinct varieties. Generally, hybrids either
cannot reproduce or their offspring are of very poor quality.
Thus, farmers using hybrid seed cannot save their seed--they
must buy new seed each year. Although high-yielding, non-
sterile varieties could be developed, the seed companies
have a disincentive for doing so since it would mean large-
scale loss of markets--and, therefore, income and profits.

Transnational agribusiness is very much in control of
the direction of ongoing and future research on seeds technologies. IRRI and CIMMYT and the nine other international
research institutes are now part of an international consortium or network under the centralized control of the Consul-
tative Group on International Agricultural Research (CGIAR).
The eleven research institutes receive funds and instruc-
tions from CGIAR and the industrial country donor agencies
which support the CGIAR network.

Ernest Feder may be provocative in the way he phrases
the problem but is hardly guilty of overstatement when he
contends that "all their research is directed exclusively
toward benefiting transnational agribusiness corporations.
Regardless whether they sell inputs or produce, process and
trade commodities, or whether they dispense agricultural
credit, agribusiness firms or banks are fully behind CGIAR,
IRRI and CIMMYT and the other nine research stations."[8]

The influence of transnational agribusiness does not
stop with research. Writing from the UP Law Center, Ernest

Feder traces their influence upon national development
policies and programs:

> Third World countries' national agricultural
> policies and programs are not any more of the
> home-grown variety. They are on the contrary
> conceived and hatched by international agribusi-
> ness monopoly capital. For every agricultural
> program in the Philippines or elsewhere, we have
> to "look under the bed," so to speak, to see who
> is hidden there. The chances are 99.9% that it
> is international monopoly capital. These poli-
> cies and programs look worldwide like broilers
> produced by a Bank of America-financed broiler
> production plant: they are all alike in looks,
> weight, size, color and taste. The policies and
> programs must all be alike because monopoly cap-
> ital operates in a uniform manner worldwide.
> Almost regardless of historical background, tra-
> dition or ecology, the structure and performance
> of Third World agricultures have come to look
> more and more alike under the impact of monopoly
> capital in expansion.[9]

Transnational elites have been quick to find partners
among the elites in Third World countries. The Green Revolution enabled the introduction of technical inputs into an
unequal system of landholdings, thereby reinforcing the gap
between rich and poor. Moreover, the Green Revolution set in
motion new forces of impoverishment, thereby not only reinforcing but even increasing the gap. Poor farmers, unable to
use the new technology, have found it increasingly difficult
to compete with the big farmers and have gone "out of business." In many areas of the Third World, this has literally
meant starvation for the peasant.

Meanwhile, large landholdings devoted to the new seeds
have grown even larger. Ironically, many areas where food
crop yields have grown the fastest are also areas that have
the fastest growing malnutrition rates. The power of the

larger landowners in India, for example, has become almost
unchallengeable. One indication of their political power
and influence is provided by the inability of the Indian
government to impose a land tax (or a tax on agricultural
income) on the beneficiaries of huge public expenditure on
irrigation, credit subsidies, subsidized seed, and fertilizer. In most Third World countries the rural scene is
typified by fake land reforms, exploitative credit systems,
even more exploitative production contracts, and high-handed
and antisocial business activities of foreign agribusiness
firms in connivance with local partners and officials.

The Coming Seed Revolution:
Forewarned Is Forearmed?

As the Green Revolution has demonstrated, if you control the seed, you are a long way to controlling the entire
food system: what crops will be grown, what inputs will be
used, and where the products will be sold. It appears that
control of the world seed industry will represent the second
phase of the Green Revolution.

There are many signs of a coming seed revolution. As
in the early 1960s, the transnational chemical industry is
in some difficulties, beset by health and safety issues.
Old products, shown to be dangerous, are being removed from
the market in industrialized countries (and to the extent
possible, being dumped in Third World markets). New products are subjected to rigorous testing, spread over several
years. Agrichemicals are facing growing public scrutiny:
concern that nitrogen fertilizers erode the ozone layer;
that biocides cause mutations in crops and people; that bio-
cide residue build-up within the body will increase cancer

risks.

By contrast, the seed industry has largely avoided attack by consumer, ecological, and regulatory bodies. The chemical industry is increasingly viewing seed as a delivery system for chemicals. Recently, many seed companies have been bought up by transnational chemical companies. In fact, over 800 seed companies have been acquired by, or have made contractual arrangements with, TNCs in the last decade.[10] There are several reasons for this. In the first place, the seed industry with a profit rate of 15 percent and an annual global sales of U.S. $10 billion (in 1978) is a profitable business. Agrichemical firms, besieged by government regu- lations (at least during the pre-Reagan period) and buyer resistance, are looking to the seed industry both to provide some profit protection and because they view seed as a valu- able deliverer of chemicals. Moreover, companies with a "chemicals" background are well equipped to move into seed genetics and become key actors in a future "genetics-supply industry."

The portents are strong for a second coming of the Green Revolution (or a seeds' revolution) which, in the words of Ernest Feder, "might mean the final chapter in the survival of millions of peasants." In preparing for this onslaught, peasant organizations, public interest and con- sumer groups, and government agencies in Third World coun- tries might do well to keep firmly in mind some of the key lessons so painfully learned from the first phase of the Green Revolution:

    a)   Overemphasis on "purely technical" solu-
          tions is both misplaced and misleading.
          Technology is not really neutral.

b) The influences of transnational agribusiness
    are pervasive and range from the more dis-
    creet and subtle to the most overt and bla-
    tant. Regulation of transnational business
    must be a priority for Third World govern-
    ments. But the stakes involved are too high
    to leave the matter to governments alone.
    The rural poor must mobilize and organize
    for the inevitable confrontation with agri-
    business, and public interest groups must
    maximize their support for efforts to curb
    and contain their onslaught.

c) Very severe international constraints on
    Third World governments limit their capac-
    ity for autonomous decision making with re-
    gard to national agricultural policies and
    programs. The rural poor must mobilize and
    develop countervailing power, both to secure
    the accountability of their own governments
    and to influence and shape the redesign of
    the policies of their governments. Public
    interest and consumer organizations have
    important intermediary roles to play in this
    regard.

d) Attempts by Third World governments to re-
    distribute resources through bureaucrat-
    ically administered programs will inevitably
    fail and end up being captured by the more
    powerful and dominant rural elites. Govern-
    ments intending to undertake such programs
    must, if they are serious about redistribu-
    tion, turn increasingly to organizations of
    the intended beneficiaries to administer
    such programs.

e) Technical solutions to the problems of
    agricultural productivity will inevitably
    end up exacerbating gaps between rich and
    poor unless preceded by structural reforms.
    Such reforms are needed to address both his-
    torical inequities of land tenure and wealth
    as well as more recent inequities resulting
    from penetration by transnational agri-
    business.

Appropriate Technologies in Seed:
Some Third World Perspectives

Obviously, specific conditions and specific needs
(short term or otherwise) will dictate "appropriateness" for
each country in the Third World. However, to a greater or
lesser extent, appropriate seed technologies for the Third
World would need to emphasize the following seed characteristics:

-- hardiness;

-- disease resistance (preferably as a result
   of multilining rather than biocides); and

-- perennials or hybrids capable of reproducing
   themselves.

Third World governments, seeking to elaborate national
agricultural policies, will need to strike a balance between
several needs:

-- the needs of farmers to grow a safe crop and
   at low cost;

-- the needs of consumers to have adequate and
   continuous supplies at a reasonable price;
   and

-- the need to secure greater profitability to
   the farmer/producer rather than transnationals.

Perhaps the most significant aspects of seed technology
choices in Third World countries relate to the distribution,
income, and nutrition effects of the technology. If reaching
and helping the smaller, poorer farmers and the poorer rural
people is an objective, then the following characteristics
might be appropriate:

a) Preference for stable over unstable seed.
    Poorer farmers find it difficult enough to
    obtain seed. If they once obtain a stable
    seed, they can replant from their own re-
    sources, year to year, without loss of
    yield.

b) Higher-yielding varieties of the food crops
    grown and eaten by the poorer sections of
    the community (e.g., millets) can be ex-
    pected to benefit them disproportionately.
    Thus, the choice of crop to which to devote
    seed-breeding expertise may itself benefit,
    to a greater or lesser extent, the poorer
    rural communities.

c) Preference for varieties with high yields
    of calories under conditions of low fertil-
    ity will favor the poorer farmers who have
    more difficulty obtaining fertilizers.

d) Water-stress tolerance will benefit those
    less well-endowed farmers whose fields are
    likely to be short of water.

e) Short-duration varieties may dispropor-
    tionately benefit farmers who are unable to
    plant on schedule because of inability to
    obtain inputs.

f) Varieties with a high return to labor-
    intensity may favor poorer farmers who can
    rely on their family labor with negligible
    opportunity cost.

g) Varieties which will fit into existing tra-
    ditional farming systems and existing or
    anticipated farm labor demand profiles will
    tend to benefit the poorer, smaller men who
    are unable or less able than their better-
    off neighbors to attract or pay casual
    labor.

h) Varieties which can be interplanted with
    other crops to reduce risk and increase

       calorie yields (and perhaps nitrogen fixa-
tion) may benefit those with very small
plots of land.

(i) Varieties which are independent of mechan-
ical requirements will reduce dependence on
those who monopolize tractors or other ma-
chines. A variety of rice grown in Sri
Lanka (H.4), for all its other excellence,
is difficult to husk without a tractor.
This requirement increased the dependence
of smaller farmers on richer ones.

The above itemization is meant to illustrate that
policy choices do exist to bias technology in favor of the
very poor. The decision to make such a bias will, of
course, be a political one. In India, at least, precedents
for building such a bias into technology development and
dissemination are found in the national policy toward community bio-gas plants and village woodlots. The present surge
in prices of petroleum-based agrichemicals provides economically rational reasons to break away from the technology of
agribusiness, and governments truly wishing to try to benefit their rural poor are now uniquely able to invoke economic justifications for policies which are less beneficial
to rural elites.

To sum up, decisions about policies and priorities
regarding seed-breeding are so vital in terms of their distribution, income, and nutrition effects that seed-breeding
is too important to be left to the seed-breeders. Decisions
regarding seed-breeding must be opened up to more public
view and apparaisal.

Seed technologies *can* be biased to disproportionately
benefit the rural poor. Indeed one might well argue, given
the growing disillusionment with political and administrative

measures for reaching the poorer rural people, that seed-breeding priorities and policies *should* be so biased. However, one fact remains inescapable. Transnational agribusinesses are certainly not the appropriate vehicles for developing such technologies. Large, centralized TNCs have little experience, expertise, or even interest in developing and marketing products to low-income, highly dispersed consumers with unfamiliar tastes and habits. Third World countries must indeed turn elsewhere for appropriate seed technologies.

It is also doubtful that Third World countries can look to the international agricultural research system for appropriate seeds technology. Another significant international institution is the Food and Agriculture Organization (FAO) in Rome which has established a Seed Improvement and Development Program (SIDP). Excerpts of SIDP advice to Third World policy makers indicate the contribution that SIDP has been making to promoting the global seed industry:

> While the government always has an important role in the development of the seed program, it should not be monopolistic or exclusive. Participation of the nongovernment sector in seed production and marketing should be actively encouraged through initiatives such as special credit, tax concessions, lease purchase arrangements for facilities and equipment, low rental land, technical assistance, relaxation of restrictions on landholding and accessibility to basic seed stocks of publicly-developed cultivars....
> Farmers should be supplied, as soon as possible, with a package of balanced inputs including quality seeds, fertilizers, water, plant protection chemicals and machinery in order to obtain higher yields.[11]

This "package approach," of vital importance to the
global seed industry, has been a source of considerable
concern for many Third World scientists.

The SIDP has also been at the forefront in terms of
encouraging Third World governments to subsidize agrichemical inputs and basic seed prices.

*Alternative Seeds Technologies for
the Third World: Prospects Dim or
Otherwise?*

This brief review of the global seed industry and the
international agricultural research system makes it clear
that if Third World governments are interested in the development of alternative seeds technologies they must, in the
main, "do it themselves." Some tentative propositions are
offered to initiate such a process of self-reliance:

a) SIDP advice to the contrary, the government
    sector in seed production and marketing must
    be strengthened.

b) Small, national private-sector seed firms
    may be encouraged (as suggested by SIDP) but
    only if they are not linked in any way to
    the global seed industry. The reason for
    such delinking is not phobia regarding trans-
    nationals. A more pragmatic reason exists
    for delinking--namely, the technology of the
    transnationals, emphasizing uniformity and
    biased against the poor, is inappropriate to
    most Third World needs.

c) Within the UN system, Third World countries
    must negotiate the position that interna-
    tional development assistance for seed tech-
    nology development is not to be channelled
    solely through the CGIAR network. Direct
    support for Third World national activities

(in fields of both crop research and genetic conservation) must be recognized as a legitimate contender for financial assistance under the UN system.

d) Third World host governments must attempt to regain some degree of national control over the International Agricultural Research Centres (IARCs) located in their countries.

e) IARCs must increasingly emphasize Third World needs rather than those of the global seed industry. In fact, greater accountability of the entire system of International Agricultural Research must be a goal Third World countries continue to strive for.

f) Within Third World countries, farmers' organizations, consumer associations, and public interest groups must all act as "watchdogs" and critique and reassess national agricultural policies in general and "technical" decisions about plant-breeding priorities and policies in particular.

g) Sympathetic professional activists in Third World countries should begin to explore ways in which they pool their interest and abilities to achieve greater cumulative impact. An interesting example of such an effort in America is provided by the Frank Porter Graham Demonstration Farm and Educational Center which is run by the National Sharecroppers Fund and which tries "to advance the best interests of the nation's sharecroppers, tenant farmers, migrant workers and small farmers."

h) Greater participation by the poorer farmers in determining seed priorities and policies must be accepted as being not merely a means but also an end in itself.

Efforts to develop alternative seed technologies in Third World countries will not go very far unless, as Pat

Mooney cautions, three major myths are exploded:

a) the myth that the "population explosion"
   threatens our food resources and makes
   necessary the kind of draconian development strategies evidenced by the Green
   Revolution;

b) the myth that the First World has the
   answer to increased food security through
   high energy-input food production technologies; and

c) the myth that agrichemical companies will
   bring innovation and creativity to plant
   breeding rather than uniformity and chemical dependence.[12]

It is much too readily accepted that seed is an international commodity. Many of the Third World's problems are
caused by this kind of conception of seed and perhaps we
need to move back to a conception of seed as a national commodity which moves across international boundaries (only
with caution) if in the genuine interests of the world's
poor and hungry. Only then can the promise of the Green
Revolution--to feed the world's hungry--cease to be hypoc-
risy or worse.

Notes

1. Ernest Feder in preface to Rene E. Ofreneo, *Capitalism
   in Philippine Agriculture,* Quezon City: Foundation for
   Nationalist Studies, 1980, p. v.

2. Arthur Moser cited in Pat Roy Mooney, *Seeds of the
   Earth,* Ottawa: Canadian Council for International Cooperation, 1979, p. 40.

3. Cited in Mooney, *op. cit.,* p. 43.

4. Dr. Norman Myers cited in Mooney, *op. cit.*, p. 37.

5. Mooney, *op. cit.*, p. 41.

6. *The Wall Street Journal*, June 14, 1972, p. 1, cited in Mooney, *op. cit.*, pp. 37-38.

7. *U.S. News and World Report*, cited in Mooney, *op. cit.*, p. 41.

8. Feder in Ofreneo, *op. cit.*, p. v.

9. Ibid., pp. v-vi.

10. Pat Roy Mooney, "The Law of the Seed: Another Development and Plant Genetic Resources," *Development Dialogue*, 1983: 1-2, p. 96.

11. Mooney, *Seeds of the Earth*, *loc. cit.*, pp. 48-49.

12. Ibid., p. 103.

References

Literature focusing on the problems of the Third World is relatively scarce. Among such literature drawn upon in this chapter, special mention must be made of the works of Ernest Feder (e.g., *The Rape of the Peasantry*, New York: Anchor Books, 1971); Robert Chambers, Andrew Pearse, Cynthia Alcantara, Ingrid Palmer, and Rene Ofreneo. On land tenure problems, see Clair Whittemore of Oxfam. The recent research undertaken by the Agency for Community Education Services (ACES) in Nueva Ecija in the Philippines, under their High-Yielding Varieties Participatory Research and Action Program, also provided useful background.

TECHNOLOGY TO AID THE POOR: CONSTRAINTS
TO ACCESS RESULTING FROM PRIVATIZATION--
THE CASE OF BIOTECHNOLOGY

David Dembo, Clarence Dias, and Ward Morehouse

Developing Countries and Frontier
Technologies

Various emerging or frontier technologies have the
potential to benefit developing countries and the poorest
in those countries in both the urban industrial and rural
agricultural sectors.   These same technologies will also
have negative consequences for many developing countries
and especially for economically vulnerable groups in those
countries.

Thus, the microelectronics industry has provided a
market for developing countries' exports of assembled com-
ponents, creating a limited number of employment opportunities in these countries.   This same technology makes it
possible, however, to reduce employment through automation
in industries which utilize the final products.   The direct
impact is to eliminate jobs in such industries in developing countries, even though those countries have substantial
labor surpluses.   The indirect impact on the Third World is
through worker displacement in industrialized countries,
which increases chronic or structural unemployment and leads
to greater protectionism against manufactured imports from
"low-wage" developing countries.

The extent to which developing countries are able to benefit from frontier technologies (at least to an extent that will help to balance some of the dislocations caused by these same technologies) is in large part determined by the ways in which these technologies are developed in industrialized and developing countries.

While developing countries may not have much of a voice in influencing directly the development of technologies in industrialized countries, there are some possibilities for influencing the actors involved in such development indirectly--through controlling demand for products of such Research and Development (R and D) by control of inputs, especially raw materials. There are, however, other options for developing countries which might allow them to avoid some of the negative impacts of these developments through strengthening domestic capabilities in R and D or through cooperation with other developing countries.

Constraints on Access to Technology:
Privatization

Of greatest concern to those wishing to influence the development of frontier technologies in ways which would benefit developing countries (and especially the poor in these countries) should be the growing trend toward privatization in the North (not, however, absent in the South-- especially between developing countries). By privatization, we refer to a variety of processes which result in a resource, a product, or a technology being moved from out of the public domain (i.e., in principle, the commons where they would have been available to anyone anywhere with the capacity to use them) and into the control (and often the owner-

ship) of private hands, be they individual or corporate.
Privatization *ipso facto* restricts access. What was freely
accessible earlier becomes, as a result of privatization,
either totally inaccessible or accessible only under restricted conditions which are often onerous and usually more
costly. Thus, privatization represents the negation of
free, open, or public access.

But "privatization," as we use the term here, does not
necessarily refer to the "private sector." While the process of privatization does result in greater roles for the
private sector, those who engage in privatization include
public sector research institutions and donor agencies funding research and reserving patent rights to themselves. In
many developing countries, large public sector enterprises
are being created in order to be strong partners in joint
ventures with transnational corporations in order to provide
a countervailing force or alternative to such transnational
corporations. Usually, these large state enterprises operate under a legal and regulatory framework which enables
them to engage in privatization to the same or even greater
extent than their private sector or transnational counterparts. Although they are *public* corporations, their operational ethos is very much that of the private sector.

Privatization may be the result of various characteristics of the development of a technology. In some cases,
there are inherent aspects of the technology which make
secrecy and privatization possible. As an example, hybrid
seed varieties contain their own built-in protection since
their duplication is impossible without knowledge of their
parent lines, which knowledge can be easily kept secret by
those marketing the seed.

Market forces also dictate a course of secrecy. It is standard commercial practice for transnational corporations to be secretive about the exact nature of research they are conducting to maintain their competitive positions. The creation of property rights (under, for example, patent legislation) provides a very strong motive for privatization. Rights of ownership and control are vital, both in establishing market monopolies and in preserving existing market monopolies. For example, a company can preempt entry into the market of a rival product by obtaining a patent on the product and not working the patent.

Privatization in industrialized countries poses at least two major obstacles to the beneficial introduction of products, based on frontier technology, into developing countries. Free and open discourse among scientists has long characterized interactions between such persons in universities and other institutions in and among both industrialized and developing countries. With the growing trend toward privatization, and especially with increased corporate funding of and influence on university research and hiring by private enterprises of university and other research institute scientists, such open communication is being jeopardized. This would have a negative impact on the ability of developing country scientists to benefit from R and D in industrialized countries.

The second obstacle posed by privatization is a result of the shift in direction of R and D to a search for products based primarily on profit potential. This is especially crucial for the least developed countries and for the poor in all countries. These groups are the least able to pay for and provide a market for products they need. Thus, R and D

directed by profit criteria will not be directed toward
products needed primarily by such persons. As research in
public sector institutions is increasingly tied up with
corporate funding and control, or with support of government agencies which encourage the privatization through
patenting of research results with "commercial" potential,
this aspect of privatization will be exacerbated.

These two obstacles of privatization are apparent in
developments in several frontier technologies. In the next
section, we examine a case study of privatization in biotechnology (as one of the more important frontier technologies)--its historical development, consequences for developing countries, and especially the poor in these countries.
In a final section of the paper, we explore possible strategies for dealing with privatization.

Privatization in Biotechnology

Biotechnology offers tremendous promise for developing
countries over a wide range of products and applications.
Biotechnology has the potential for helping to solve a
number of the major problems that are endemic in developing
countries, particularly those relating to human and animal
health and those relating to shortages of food and energy.
Thus, most developing countries will be anxious to maximize
access to appropriate biotechnology on the most equitable
terms possible. However, such access seems likely to be
greatly restricted unless the growing trend of privatization
of biotechnology is arrested and reversed.

It is important to view the phenomenon of privatization
in its historical context in the First World and in the

Third World. Privatization occurred in the *First World* as
a result of several forces. Several large chemical transnational corporations, fearing the impacts of environmental
regulation during the 1960s, began to look for new products
that they could sell in the global markets they already
commanded. Seeds came to be viewed as a delivery mechanism
for products (such as pesticides and fertilizers) of these
companies.

Although TNCs use various means to privatize knowledge,
there is a close relationship in different industrial sectors between patent protection and market monopolies (or at
least oligopolies with substantial barriers to entry), leading to higher prices and profit margins. Plant breeders'
rights legislation (Plant Patent ACT) was originally enacted in the U.S. in 1930. This legislation covered asexu-
ally propagated plants (i.e., flowers, ornamental shrubs
and trees, and fruits). Efforts were mounted by concerned
segments of industry to extend patent or equivalent protection, first, to new plant varieties resulting from conventional plant breeding technologies through plant breeders'
rights legislation. This was followed by similar efforts
to extend such protection of products resulting from recent
advances in biotechnology.

Thus, in the U.S., the Plant Variety Protection Act was
passed in 1970, and its coverage extended in 1980. This
extension facilitated the entry of the U.S. into the International Union for the Protection of New Varieties of Plants
(UPOV). In the same year, the U.S. Supreme Court in a land-
mark decision in the case of *Diamond* vs. *Chakrabarty* found
that live, laboratory-modified microorganisms were patentable. Prior to that decision, living creatures had

generally been excluded from the domain of patentable material and could not be converted into private property
through patent law. But the one major exception to this
position--namely, patent-like protection for living plant
varieties--played an important role in the U.S. Supreme
Court's decision.

The net effect of these developments is that, within
the past decade and a half in the U.S. (with varying periods
in other industrialized countries), legislation and litigation have removed from the public domain, and converted
into private property, strains of varieties of plants and
microorganisms.

In the *Third World*, the spread of privatization has
occurred for several reasons. In the agricultural sector
in recent decades, most developing country governments,
faced with a crucial need to step up domestic food production, have turned to high-yielding varieties (HYVs) of crops.
The term "high-yielding" is misleading. These varieties are,
in fact, only more responsive to inputs of fertilizers, pesticides, and water. Without such inputs they often yield
less than traditional varieties, and are more susceptible to
disease and weather conditions. Such varieties have been
more aptly termed "high-response," or "input-intensive."

The HYVs have often been supplied by large transnational corporations, usually active not only in the seeds
industry but also in the petroleum and chemical industries
as well, in connection with which they manufacture and
market other inputs necessary for HYVs to live up to their
name, such as fertilizers and pesticides. Developing
countries have usually had (and continue to have) very weak
regulatory and administrative mechanisms to deal with the

day-to-day operations of transnational corporations after
they have been let into the country. A variety of malprac-
tices (including privatization) have occurred as a result.

Moreover, developing country governments have (at times
unwittingly and at other times in direct collusion) facilitated the market penetration of transnational corporations
by including the products of the TNCs in a "package" delivered by government agencies, comprising credit, water,
fertilizers, pesticides, seeds, and extension services. A
few developing countries have even succumbed to pressures
and adopted plant patenting and plant breeders' rights legislation. Also, so far as the industrial sector has been
concerned, many developing countries have been forced to
permit privatization in order to gain access to needed technology from transnational corporations. These countries
have been compelled to provide patent protection of such
technologies since the transnational corporations would re-
fuse to grant access to its technology unless such patent
protection were granted. For the transnational corporation,
of course, patent protection and property rights are the key
to securing market monopolies and thereby ensuring higher
prices and profit margins.

Because virtually all of the more advanced R and D in
biotechnology is being conducted in a handful of industrialized countries (with the greatest concentration in Japan
and the U.S.), it has been difficult for developing countries to resist the spread of privatization in biotechnology.
Indeed, present trends suggest that it is going to be more,
not less, difficult to resist these pressures in the years
ahead, unless the thrust towards greater privatization in
industrialized countries can be arrested and reversed and/or

some Third World countries can develop an independent capacity in key areas of advanced biotechnologies.

Social Impacts in Developing Countries
of Privatization of Biotechnology

Proponents of privatization in First World countries
argue that patent or patent-like protection would benefit
developing countries. They argue that patents (and the royalty fees they bring with them) provide an incentive for
greater private sector investment in the development and
commercialization of new technologies. They contend that
private control of certain technologies will both enhance
and speed up their dissemination and application. Greater
involvement of the commercial sector in First World countries, it is urged, results in such dissemination of new advances in technology because commercial concerns must market
their products as rapidly and widely as possible if they are
to survive and prosper. Rather than argue the merits of
such contentions, we would prefer to examine instead some of
the social impacts that result from the introduction into
developing countries of *privatized technology* by transnational corporations and some of the societal consequences,
for developing countries, of privatization of biotechnology
in industrialized countries.

(1) Impacts on R and D Priorities--Application and
Commercialization:

Approximately two dozen transnational corporations who
play a predominant role in manufacturing and marketing
pharmaceuticals and petrochemicals are in the forefront of

the biorevolution. This fact, coupled with the increasing private and proprietary character of biotechnology research in the First World, raises several crucial concerns for the Third World.

The dominant role played by the transnational corporations in biotechnology R and D will inevitably lead to skewed research priorities that are determined by and subordinate to their own global strategies. The directions which the present development of biotechnology processes and products has taken thus far are determined largely by the commercial potential of the products and processes and the size of their anticipated markets. Major investment has been made in the development of products for which a significant demand exists from consumers who are able to pay--and, even better, pay well--for such products.

There has been relatively less concern for products of interest primarily to developing countries because even though the demand may be great, they cannot pay enough. Biomass conversion technologies are, at present, not economically attractive to biotechnology companies in the industrialized countries even though they are of great importance to developing countries. Many of the pressing needs of developing countries are ideal subjects for modern biotechnology: vaccines against tropical diseases, protein-rich food sources, alternative energy, and pollution control. But the only areas of R and D being pursued are those which will presumably bring substantial returns to investors. The problem of bringing the benefits of biotechnology to the Third World remains acute and seems unlikely to be solved unless the Third World can develop indigenous biotechnological capabilities.

Corporate strategies can also influence the pace of commercialization of the applications of biotechnology R and D. Thus, for example, a malaria vaccine which had already been developed at the laboratory stage and was ready for scaling up to the production stage has been held up for several months, initially because the company chosen to produce the vaccine--Genentech--refused to do so without an exclusive license (which ran counter to the policies of W.H.O., one of the original funders of the project) and subsequently while the parties responsible for developing the vaccine searched for another company to produce and market it. This search is no doubt being made more difficult by the fact that those most in need of the vaccine are least able to pay for it.

(2) Impacts on Access to R and D:

Privatization has led to increasing secrecy surrounding biotechnology research. Researchers in most private industries are restrained in the discussion of their work by corporate policies that seek to keep R and D results secret, and by the strictures against public disclosure of patentable knowledge before it is patented. Commercialization of skills and know-how is being accompanied by an enlarging secrecy around the knowledge base of discovery. This is not only true of research being undertaken in the private, commercial sector, but is also beginning to affect research being undertaken in univerities. The increasing treatment of science as a commodity and the growing industry/university linkages in the First World have endangered the traditional concepts of free access to the results of scientific research being undertaken within an "open global community of scholars" and evaluations thereof by this community. Contractual arrangements for biotechnology research entered into by transnational corporations with universities have led to situations of potential conflict of interest.

There is growing need in the First World to evolve guidelines which will ensure that the university remains a place for open, free, and objective inquiry and that public funds are used by the universities in the public interest. From the Third World point of view, this trend in the First World of co-optation by transnational corporations of public sector research institutions is justifiably alarming as yet another mechanism for reinforcing the trend towards privatization of biotechnology.

As far as R and D directed toward plant varieties and crops is concerned, privatization has had an impact on access to the following:

a) germplasm and plant genetic resources essential to further plant breeding work and tissue culture research;

b) elite breeding lines which are used in the development of new plant varieties;

c) new commercial plant varieties, and in the case of tissue culture research, new products and new applications and uses of products; and

d) scientific and technological processes which have created c) above.

(3) Impacts on Access to Technology:

Privatization inevitably creates *problems of access*. Technology which was accessible earlier becomes, as a result of privatization, either totally inaccessible or accessible under restricted conditions which are usually more difficult and costly. For the Third World, in addition to lack of or

restricted access, privatization leads to the perpetuation
of technological dependencies, inappropriateness of "packaged" technologies, and inequities regarding the costs and
terms on which access to such "privatized" technologies can
be secured.

Agriculture provides the best example of the negative
impacts of privatization on access to appropriate technology.
Because of the dominant role played by chemical transnationals in agricultural R and D, such technology as is now
available is proving to be highly inappropriate. It is be-
coming more and more apparent, in Third World and First
World alike, that the kind of chemically intensive agriculture which privatization aids and abets is poisoning ground-
water supplies, denuding the soil of its organic nutrients,
and leaving unacceptably high residues of toxic substances
embedded in the food chain, the output of which is ultimately consumed by human beings.

(4) Impacts on Environment:

In addition to the harmful environment of chemical-
intensive agriculture, privatization of biotechnology raises
many concerns for environmentalists. Initially, the dangers
resulting from biohazards may have been greatly exaggerated
to the point of near hysteria. Today, however, even after a
more dispassionate appraisal, there remains clear need for
regulation of biotechnology research and application to
protect the environment. This area has proved to be fraught
with difficulty, both because of the secrecy surrounding biotechnology research and because the solution proposed by
those in industry--of self-regulation through an industry-
devised code--is not likely to provide adequate protection

to the public if past experience with the food, drug, and agricultural chemical industries is any guide. Self-regulation tends to work only when opportunities for conflict between industry self-interests and societal interests are few, or when external factors compel industry to adopt a position of enlightened self-interest. This does not appear to be the case with biotechnology so far.

Many may feel that, in the Third World, regulation may be less important because of the pervasive and dominant role of the public sector in this area. But, as the experience with nuclear energy has shown, it is unwise to assume that assumption by government of a function necessarily obviates or decreases need for regulatory controls. An additional aspect of regulation will be involved in Third World countries and this aspect relates to regulation of TNCs since transnational corporations will, inevitably, play a dominant role regarding the introduction of such technologies into the Third World.

These environmental/regulatory aspects need to be seriously addressed because, while initially transnational corporation investment in biotechnology was primarily in the field of health (an area which is in general adequately regulated, at least in the First World), the present investment emphasis is on agriculture (an area which is much less stringently regulated in the First World and is largely unregulated in Third World countries).

In addition, the military applications of biotechnology have important environmental and societal implications which need urgent examination by social action groups and regulatory agencies. While advanced military-related biotechnology is being developed primarily in the First World, its impacts

are, of course, worldwide. Such military applications are
of concern to a growing number of groups in the First World,
and need to be closely examined for their potential impacts
on the Third World.

(5) Impacts on Values and Lifestyles:

Privatization tends to encourage values of secrecy and
self-interest. Scientific research ceases to be an intellectual endeavor pursued within an open global community of
scholars. Instead, science becomes a commodity to be traded
for maximum profit in a global market. Thus, public sector
plant breeding research in the past proceeded from a deep
commitment to cooperation and scientific exchange. It used
to be true that plant breeding knew no borders and united
plant geneticists all over the world. However, with the advent of plant patenting and the resulting privatization,
today private sector plant breeding takes place in a highly
competitive setting and is inevitably designed to meet business criteria and corporate plans. The existing bias in
plant breeding favoring chemicals has inevitable impact on
societal values relating to ecology.

Privatization causes "brain drain," both from Third
World to First World countries, and also within Third World
and First World countries alike--from public sector research
institutions to corporate research laboratories. Privatization and the potential for substantial financial reward it
holds out tend to inhibit the development of an indigenous
scientific community in developing countries. Many scientists are likely to aim their research more toward an international audience than toward national or local priorities.
They tend to seek evaluation and recognition of their work

through an international professional peer-group review
system and this, at times, leads to a colonization of intellectual activity.

Privatization also affects lifestyles in various ways.
Large transnational corporations offer Third World scientists financial terms so lucrative that resistance becomes
difficult. This, in turn, enables them to become accustomed
to a lifestyle far more affluent than what they could expect
if they returned to their native countries. The situation
is exacerbated when expatriate technical experts, working
for a transnational corporation in a Third World country,
carry with them a lifestyle which is much too ostentatious
in the host country. The creation of an elite group of
"white brahmins" and "brown brahmins," completely dependent
on corporate largesse, tends to weaken further the international open community of scholars needed to ensure free
access to technological innovation. Privatization also encourages within the larger community a lifestyle based on
conspicuous consumption. For privatization to bring financial rewards, new commodities and new products based upon
applications of the privatized research must be consistently
brought into the market.

(6) Impacts of Privatization on the Poor and on
     Income Distribution:

Most developing countries are faced with a highly
inequitable pattern of income distribution with growing pauperization of the majority of their peoples. Privatization
tends to exacerbate further this problem of the increasing
gap between rich and poor in developing countries. As noted
above, biotechnology R and D in the First World is unlikely
to address the needs of the poor in developing countries.

In First World countries, because R and D costs are very
high, they can only be amortized by product applications
which command high prices. There is little financial incentive to concentrate on research benefiting the poor.

Moreover, because of the secrecy surrounding research
that privatization brings about, certain research processes
capable of being adopted to help meet survival needs are
kept privatized because the same processes are being used in
commercial applications from which the corporation sponsor-
ing the research hopes to benefit greatly. There are also
instances of transnational corporations obtaining patents
for products which benefit the consumer, but not working the
patent because such product would displace existing products
of the corporation already resulting in high profits. Finally, privatization of biotechnology is also likely to aug-
ment the "refraction effect" through which the introduction
of new technologies in the Third World increases disparities
between the rich and the poor, as experience with the introduction of other new technologies in the Third World including the Green Revolution clearly bears out.

(7) Impacts on Public Sector Institutions:

Privatization of biotechnology also seriously affects
public sector institutions in both Third and First World
countries. In First World countries, there is growing concern about adverse consequences resulting from university/
industry linkages in biotechnology. There also concern
being expressed in some countries in Europe (notably Great
Britain) that public sector research institutions are increasingly being limited to the role of undertaking basic
research which is then used by private sector institutions

to yield commercial applications. In such countries, there is now growing demand for fiscal and other policies which will strengthen public sector institutions and enable them to be competitive with the corporate sector.

So far as public sector institutions in the Third World are concerned, privatization has, as noted above, created problems of secrecy. Thus, for example, the government tea research institute in Sri Lanka has experienced difficulty in obtaining breeding materials from its counterpart in India. Both India and Sri Lanka are competing for a limited export market in tea, and India fears that tissue culture research in Sri Lanka is at a stage where it might provide a breakthrough, giving Sri Lanka a definite edge in the export market.

Privatization of biotechnology has also created a need in the Third World for strengthening and, at times, creating new public sector institutions to deal with both production and regulation. Moreover, given the pervasive and signif-icant nature of the societal impacts of applications of bio-technology, there is also a need (underscored by the priva-tized nature of biotechnology) for enhancing the participa-tory nature of Third World policy-making institutions deal-ing with biotechnology. Any significant new technological innovation creates a need for institutional responses. In the case of biotechnology, this need becomes all the more important because of privatization.

(8) Impacts on Private Sector Institutions:

Privatization of biotechnology has ensured that trans-national corporations will be the main agents for introduc-ing such technology into developing countries. This will intensify the need to strengthen the negotiating capabil-

ities of the private sector in developing countries. There
are several characteristics unique to biotechnology that
offer the potential for such strengthening and it is essential that this potential be realized.

Biotechnology products are also likely to cause serious
displacement of traditional products in Third World countries. The need is thus created for effective policies of
"adjustment assistance" or protection of "infant industries"
to minimize the disruptive effects of such displacements and
dislocations.

(9) Impacts on International Development Cooperation:
The privatized nature of biotechnology makes it all the
more vital that mechanisms be created to ensure developing
country access to biotechnology through international development cooperation. One such initiative has been launched
with the creation of the International Centre for Genetic
Engineering and Biotechnology (ICGEB). Because of the privatization of biotechnology, however, there will be severe
pressures to limit the effectiveness of ICGEB since a strong
ICGEB would prove a formidable rival to transnational corporations as an alternative source for developing country
access to biotechnology. Hence, Third World efforts must be
directed toward strengthening ICGEB and guarding against its
being co-opted by the private sector in the industrialized
countries.

(10) Impacts on Third World Dependency:
The use of technology to foster dependency relationships has been repeatedly documented. It is clear that at
least one industrialized country (the U.S.) intends to
foster dependency through the privatization of biotechnology.

A major government study of U.S. competitive positions in biotechnology makes this revealing comment: "America's leadership in high technology is the foundation upon which much of our contemporary national security strategy and commercial advantage lies.... It has been a matter of concern that the transfer of biotechnology abroad might jeopardize America's scientific and commercial leadership and national security interests."[1] This aspect of privatization will intensify as countries seek to maintain their competitive positions in biotechnology in both the First and Third World.

The Search for Strategies to Deal with Privatization of Biotechnology

Privatization of biotechnology will create problems of lack of or restricted access, perpetuation of technological dependencies, inappropriateness of "packaged" technologies, and inequities regarding the costs and terms on which access to such "privatized" technologies can be secured. Privatization also reinforces trends toward vertical integration among transnational giants with concentration of production and marketing in a very limited number of companies. Privatization has led to tensions in academic/industry relations, disputes as to who really owns the scientist's work, and "brain drain."

Thus, strategies need to be evolved in the Third World and industrialized countries alike to:

a) arrest and, if possible, reverse the current trend toward greater privatization; and

b) cope with the adverse consequences resulting
    from existing privatization.

Some of these strategies can be effectively implemented unilaterally by one country alone. Others might
need collective action by like-minded countries or groups
in the Third and First World. We list below a number of
such strategies, not in a prescriptive manner, but rather
to be suggestive and illustrative:

(1) Development of indigenous capabilities in countries of the Third World. This must be accorded highest
priority and, in particular, the role of public sector institutions must be safeguarded and strengthened so that
such institutions can act as equal partners with, or provide adequate countervailing power to, First World transnational corporations operating within such countries. In
this regard, it is also vital that realistic policies be
adopted to arrest "brain drain" and effective measures be
taken to preserve the "open community of scholars" and to
protect the public interest in university/industry relationships in Third World countries.

(2) Strengthening of an international system in the
public sector (beginning with ICGEB) to parallel the private sector in the First World in order to enhance Third
World access to biotechnology.

(3) Strengthening the negotiating capacity of Third
World countries which need (in the short run at the very
least) selective linkages with the private sector in First
World countries, both in order to gain access to technology
from abroad as well as to speed up the commercialization of
indigenously developed technologies.

(4) Preventing the adoption in the Third World of

legislation permitting the patenting of products or processes of tissue culture technology and other biotechnologies. It is vital that Third World solidarity be maintained in resisting proprietization of biotechnology.
Third World countries should, with one voice, say no to the
introduction of patent law which protects biotechnology. Of
course, Third World countries with indigenous biotechnology
capabilities have a legitimate interest in safeguarding
technological innovations developed indigenously. But this
can be achieved in a variety of ways other than by creating
property rights for such innovations. Within the country
itself the author of the innovation can be rewarded through
a variety of devices: user fees, taxes on sales, fiscal
incentives, etc. A more complex problem occurs when, for
example, a new plant variety developed in Mexico, is patented in the U.S. by a U.S.-based transnational corporation
and then marketed around the world. To prevent a recur-
rence of this kind of "larceny," one possible strategy
would be for the Third World inventor to obtain patents in
the relevant First World countries, although this might
prove both expensive and burdensome.

Third World countries must take steps to secure clari-
fication of the law governing international recognition of
such patents so that patents obtained through stolen inven-
tions will be denied international protection. If Third
World countries choose the option of adopting their own
biotechnology patent laws they will be creating the last
link in the privatization process and will enable transnational corporations to secure global market monopolies for
their products. At any event, Third World countries stand
to lose more than they will gain if they join the rush to

patent.

(5) Strengthening the regulatory capabilities of the Third World.

(6) Adoption of legislative measures (such as those prescribing ceilings on royalty payments) aimed at minimizing the gains from privatization.

(7) Strengthening Third World cooperation in biotechnology. Several Third World countries (notably, Argentina, Brazil, India, Mexico, the Philippines, and Thailand) have, given high priority to developing their own national capabilities in biotechnology. This makes it possible to devise specific projects involving South/South cooperation. One of the areas where a serious effort along such lines might be worth exploring is that of setting up a collaborative biotechnology supply industry. Several Third World researchers from such countries have expressed the fear that, despite their indigenous capabilities, they may be kept dependent upon a TNC-dominated biotechnology supply industry providing raw materials, instrumentation, design, and construction of "biological" factories needed for their research.

(8) Lack of access to information often can thwart the formulation and pursuit of effective strategies. The need to gather "social intelligence" on biotechnology can hardly be stressed enough, and collaborative efforts cutting across Third World/First World lines at sharing biotechnology information should be greatly expanded where they now exist and initiated where they do not. Accurate, up-to-date information is needed by governments, institutions, and organizations, but also on legal, industrial, and socioeconomic aspects of this rapidly changing field of tech-

nology in industrialized countries.

(9) Relatively little is yet known about the variety
of techniques adopted to achieve privatization and of
strategies involving manipulation of patent laws to this
end. Research conducted, concurrently in key Third World
countries on this subject, would be of tremendous value in
efforts to evolve other strategies to deal with privatization.

Even though some aspects of biotechnology are already
in use, much of the very great potential of other areas of
biotechnology lies in the future. This potential is truly
enormous in its consequences, both positive and negative,
for the Third World. Equally large are the potential
problems resulting from the application of biotechnology
that also lie in the future. This makes it all the more
important to start now to implement strategies that will
arrest, and if possible reverse, trends such as privatization that would lead to skewed development of technology
and a perverse distribution of its benefits so that those
who need the benefits most will not once again be denied
many of these benefits because they are poor and powerless.

Note

1. *Biobusiness World Data Base* (a Draft Report by a
    U.S. Government Interagency Working Group on Com-
    petitive and Transfer Aspects of Biotechnology),
    Washington, D.C.: McGraw-Hill Publications, 1983,
    p. A-1.

References

This chapter has drawn largely on two other papers by the authors, one appearing in the first issue of the U.N. Center on Science and Technology's *ATAS* (Advance Technology Alert System) *Bulletin* entitled "Privatization and Tissue Culture Technology," and the second to appear in a report of a 1984 seminar held in Brasilia on biotechnology and its legal aspects.

While there has been much research and writing on bio-technology developments and its impact on industrialized countries, especially on comparative positions of various countries and methods to improve these positions, there is relatively little material available on impacts on the Third World. Of special interest are the writings of Jack Kloppenburg, Martin Kenney, and Fred Buttel of the Department of Rural Sociology at Cornell University, and those of Pat Roy Mooney and Cary Fowler of the Rural Advancement Fund in North Carolina. The authors of this chapter have also been engaged in studies of plant breeders' rights legislation and the role of transnational corporations in biotech-nology.

PRODUCT DISPLACEMENT: BIOTECHNOLOGY'S
IMPACTS ON DEVELOPING COUNTRIES

Clarence Dias, David Dembo, and Ward Morehouse

Despite all the publicity surrounding their development as panaceas for many of the problems confronting the world's people, especially the poor and hungry, it is increasingly evident that frontier technologies are rarely, if ever, introduced without disruptions to the economies into which they are injected or to other economies dependent on these. Thus, for example, the package of technologies which made possible the Green Revolution, as discussed in other contributions to this volume, has, despite its promise for increased food yields to feed the world's hungry, often resulted in further impoverishing the same people it was supposed to benefit.

Even as the microelectronics revolution with all of its labor-saving (read labor-displacing) characteristics is playing havoc with the employment situation in both industrialized and developing countries, a new technological revolution--even more far-reaching in its potential applications and impacts--is underway. The biotechnology revolution offers great promise for the solution of the problems of the Third World poor--eradication of hunger and disease, energy production, environmental improvements. But it has an even stronger potential for disrupting these very same segments of society. Biotechnology, as it is being developed in industrialized countries, addresses primarily First World countries: i.e., treatment for A.I.D.S., not malaria and diarrhea; crops which make possible increased use of pesticides, not crops with lower input requirements; agricultural improvements (both animal and crop) directed at export markets and cash crops, not feeding the poor.

In another chapter in this volume, the trends which have promoted these developments in R and D in biotechnology are examined. In this chapter, we examine the impacts of developments in the North on the Third World. Impacts on possibilities for export-oriented economic developments, and impacts on the poorest in these countries. These will largely be impacts from developments which the South is unable to control. This makes even more crucial the development of strategies to deal with these impacts, the subject of the second half of this chapter.

Product Displacement

Biotechnology's promise for disease control and treatment are perhaps its best known aspects. Yet the most far-reaching and immediate impacts of biotechnology will be (and, to some extent, already are) in agriculture, and more generally in raw material inputs for industry as well as in energy production and use. Because of the lengthy product development/testing/approval process for pharmaceutical products, companies are typically focusing on improving existing products rather than introducing wholly new products by lowering input cost and lessening side effects through artificial substitutes for human and animal products.

Through tissue culture technology, biotechnology makes possible rapid and precise development of crops suited to growth in far more varied environments than previously. With genetic engineering new crops are possible, as well as animals bred for increased yields with fewer inputs. Advances in reproductive technology make possible the rapid production of animals with the desired traits.

Biotechnology also provides methods for increased and more efficient production of conventional energy sources (for example, through bacteria that change the flow characteristics of oil to allow for more thorough utilization of old wells). It also provides ways of improving energy production through renewable sources such as biomass--for example, improving efficiency in the conversion of crops to alcohol, while also providing a means of increasing production of agricultural products for such conversion through methods discussed above.

Sources for energy production are not the only raw materials for which biotechnology will help to find substitutes. Substitutions will be possible, based in part on availability, dependability, and cost of the original product, for a variety of raw materials now produced in developing countries, resulting in the potential displacement of these products by substitutes produced at lowered cost or with greater quality control in industrialized countries.

Crop and product displacement will be one of the strongest and most immediate impacts of biotechnology on developing countries. Already R and D is underway to substitute products now grown, mined, or produced in developing countries with products produced more cheaply or reliably in industrialized countries. Some examples follow.

Case Studies of Product Displacement

One of the best documented cases of the displacement of
a Third World crop through advances in technology in industrialized countries is that of sugar. Sugar-producing
crops--especially sugar cane and sugar beets--are an important source of revenue and nutrition for farmers and peasants, as well as for those who process, refine, package,
export, wholesale, and retail the product in both developing
and industrialized countries. Indeed, sugar is an excellent
example of the unequal impact product displacement has on
the First and Third World. The Common Market, due to its
effective control of imports, and the U.S., through its extensive government support of agricultural prices, have been
able to lessen the impact of the displacement of sugar by
other products, whereas the loss of sugar markets in the
industrialized countries has had a highly disruptive impact
of several Third World countries.

Sugar has been displaced in recent years by high fructose corn syrup which, due in part to advances in biotechnology, can be produced economically from corn or maize for
use as an industrial sweetener in place of sugar. High fructose syrup can also be produced from potatoes or cassava.
According to a study by R. Crott (FAST Occasional Paper No.
55), in 1981 in the U.S., 1.8 million tons of imported sugar
(of a total of about 6 million tons) was displaced by high
fructose corn syrup. In Japan, some 20 percent of imported
sugar (400,000 tons) was also displaced by corn sweeteners.

This displacement has spelled disaster for sugar-
exporting countries as they no longer can control the price

or quantity of their exports. Whenever the relative price
or availability of corn makes it a preferable alternative,
the overall demand for sugar will fall. (For domestic political reasons, the U.S. is anxious to provide increased
markets for its corn production.) And this situation will
only get worse as improved techniques are developed to bring
the cost of corn syrup production down still further. In
addition, biotechnology has led to the development of aspar-
tame, an artificial sweetener with almost the same taste as
sugar and 200 times sweeter, which is taking over the market
not only from other artificial sweeteners but also from
sugar and corn sweeteners--it has about one-eighth the calories of the latter two.

Another example of the ability of industrialized
countries with a well-developed biotechnology R and D sector
to undermine developing country attempts at maintenance of
export price and volume is the case of steroid development
in Mexico. From 1950 through 1970 the primary raw materials
for producing steroid drugs (contraceptives, corticosteroids,
steroid diuretics, etc.) was barbasco, a plant grown in Mexico. Several transnational corporations, including GD
Searle, Gist-Brocades, Schering AG, Mitsubishi, and Upjohn,
have been working at various times since 1956 on developing
a synthetic alternative to the Mexican product. In the
1970s, the Mexican government sought to improve the returns
on this valuable export, but the TNCs, anticipating this
move, were able to bypass Mexican disogenin (the product of
barbasco used to produce the drugs) by relying first on a
substitute procedure, using soy sterols (from soy oil), and
then on the development of a fully synthetic substitute

manufactured through fermentation.

Recent advances in tissue culture technology make possible the industrial production of products formerly obtainable only through the gathering or harvesting of natural products, especially in developing countries. It has been estimated that natural products costing $1,000 per kilogram or more are in immediate danger of being displaced by tissue culture technology. In the longer run, products costing as little as $300 per kilo are in danger of being so displaced. In the first issue of the U.N. Center for Science and Technology for Development's *ATAS* (Advance Technology Alert System) *Bulletin*, a group of researchers at Cornell University (Martin Kenney, Jack Kloppenburg, and Frederick Buttel) provide several examples of products now being (or soon to be) developed in the laboratory through tissue culture technology to reduce costs of importing the natural product. Plants which they identify as in the process of being produced industrially include Lithospermum (from the Republic of Korea and the U.S.), Pyrethrum (Tanzania, Ecuador, and India), Papaver (Turkey), Sapota (Central America), Catharanthus (Central America), Jasminum (Central America), Digitalis (Central America), Cinchona (Indonesia), Cocoa (Brazil), and Thaumatococcus (Liberia, Ghana, and Malaysia).

In some cases, tissue culture technology will provide the means for products to be developed more economically and closer to the site where the final product (drugs, perfumes, etc.) is manufactured and from which it is marketed. In other cases, the technology will allow cheaper production of a plant in certain developing or developed countries that will, in turn, displace the products of other countries.

Developments in palm oil production provide an example

of this type of potential displacement. As Pat Roy Mooney
points out in the same issue of the *ATAS Bulletin*, Unilever,
a company with control over the advanced technologies for
propagating oil palms, now produces 500,000 oil palm plant-
lets a year in each of two facilities in the U.K. and Sing-
apore. It is possible that the company's vastly increased
production potential for palm oil at cheaper rates will
allow the company to undercut the market for many other
edible oils, although probably not corn.

Indirect Impacts

Tissue culture technology, as well as other biotechnologies, will have indirect impacts through product displacement as well. Advances in animal and plant breeding
will allow for continued increase in scale economies of production. Thus, plants which up until now could only be
grown on a small scale or were not amenable to mechanized
farming may now be redesigned for such purposes. There is
also the possibility that crops which were formerly gathered
(i.e., grew wild or not readily grown domestically) may now
be capable of domestication.

The most important indirect impacts, however, are
related to utilization of scarce resources. The introduction of products based on biotechnology, or even those meant
to offset dislocations caused by introduction of such
products elsewhere, will have important consequences for use
of land, water, fertilizers, credit, and other resources.

For example, in the Philippines during the displacements caused in the sugar/corn syrup example cited above,
the government promoted the planting of yellow maize or

corn. Corn may be used to make the syrup itself (and aid in further sugar displacement), for animal feed, for export, etc. Corn is not, however, indigenous to the Philippines and its success as a food staple, possibly displacing rice, is questionable. Whatever the results of the introduction of corn, this example shows the need to determine before-hand the impacts of alternatives--in this case, alternatives to sugar production. Is the corn using fertilizer or pesticides which might otherwise be used for crops more widely used in local diets? Is the corn to be used as animal feed, producing food for the wealthier at the expense of food production for the poor? Will corn have further impacts on size of landholdings due to its potential for mechanization and requirements for large amounts of inputs? What will be its impact on the environment--is it vulnerable to pests and diseases; does it use more chemicals than sugar-producing crops?

In alcohol for energy production, similar questions must be asked. Does the planting of sugar cane for biomass occur to the exclusion of other uses for scarce land, such as food crops? Are resources used in production of biomass being diverted from other uses?

Many of these dislocations will occur regardless of the actions of developing countries. Often the development of the technologies that make possible such product displace-ments takes place in industrialized countries, frequently in the R and D centers of TNCs of those countries. This makes the initiation of policies and programs which combat or at least ameliorate such dislocations all the more crucial.

Victims of Displacement

Displacement of products or crops through biotechnology will have a range of impacts, either direct or indirect, on developing countries and on all segments of the
population within those countries. In this section some of
the factors determining who the most effective parties will
be are discussed.

One factor which will affect the impact of displacement is the *type of product* displaced. Depending on
whether the product is primarily for export, whether it is
a cash crop or whether its primary purpose is for local consumption, the impacts will be different. If the product
being displaced is primarily for local consumption, for example, the impacts might be less far-reaching than if the
product were an important source of revenue for either the
farmer, processors, export agencies, or the government.
Even in the case of production for local consumption, however, developments of "improved" crops through tissue culture technology could have profound impact on the local
economy. The Green Revolution provides ample example of
this. Through biotechnology it will be possible to make an
ever wider range of crops dependent on herbicides and fertilizers, tying peasants even closer to chemical inputs
over the cost of which they have no control.

Other displacements can occur if, for example, a more
efficient means of growing one crop results in increased
land being utilized for that crop. In some cases, this can
result in less land for local food production. In the production of alcohol from biomass, for example, it is possible
that land otherwise used for food production will be used
instead for production of biomass to lessen the country's

dependence on imported fuel. The use of sugar cane for alcohol also results in lesser availability of this crop for local food consumption.

A second factor which will influence the impact of product or crop displacement is the nature and extent of *the related industry or services* dependent on a crop or other raw material. With the sugar example referred to above, where corn syrup is replacing a large part of the demand for sugar, there are several related industries affected by these fluctuations. These include transportation services, sugar refiners, packagers, shippers, marketers, and all of their suppliers (including suppliers to the sugar growers).

A third factor determining extent of impact is the *type of labor* involved in producing the displaced product and the character of the producers of the product and its related industries/services. If any of these affected parties involve unorganized and/or informal workers, it is less likely that strategies will be developed to help them cope with the impact of displacement than, say, if they are members of unions or are otherwise in an organized work setting.

As we have suggested, product displacement will affect all levels of developing country societies. It will affect not only the *incomes* of farmers/peasants and other raw material producers, as well as of laborers, but also the *profits* of businesses--both local and transnational--and the *revenues* of governments. It will also have an affect on consumers as local products are displaced by imported ones, as land and resources are shifted from one crop/product to another, and as new products based on the technology are introduced. Each of these direct impacts will then have secondary impacts on the other. Thus, with incomes affected by displacements, government revenues will be affected not only by import/ export considerations, but by a changed tax base and the necessity of developing strategies and programs to deal with those whose means of livelihood has been displaced.

Strategies

The negative impacts of product or crop displacement through biotechnological "advances" will be preserved and in some instances are already beginning to appear. There are five broad categories of strategies which developing countries might follow to deal with these impacts.

(1) Adjustments:

Developing countries can attempt some degree of adjustment within industries or agriculture to produce, grow, or gather different kinds of products to develop different uses for the product being displaced. They can also attempt to find new markets for their product, either in-country or through cooperation with other countries (especially developing nations). The alcohol program in Brazil provides an example of how this might occur. Sugar cane and other crops can be used for other products--in this case, production of alcohol for fuel. However, this can run into problems if land or resources otherwise used for food production are shifted to alcohol production or production of other export or luxury items.

Biotechnology might also provide the means to adjust to negative impacts caused by another of its applications. Such technology could provide a means of producing crops or products cheap enough in the original country to make industrial or other replacement products superfluous.

(2) Allocating Social Costs:

It is most likely that those who will be hardest hit by developments in biotechnology will be the poorest in developing countries. Thus, while Unilever will be growing more and more palms for palm oil, it is unlikely that the poor farmers will benefit. It is more likely that the large plantations will continue to grow, displacing land otherwise available for food. The tie-in of seeds with herbicides, pesticides, and fertilizers (facilitated through tissue culture technology) and the links between chemical TNCs and seed companies will also raise the price of food production beyond the means of many farmers (who often have no recourse to traditional varieties due to credit arrangements or simple unavailability), much as was the case with the Green Revolution.

Governments of developing countries will thus have to develop policies to help those affected, either through adjustment, as discussed above, or through direct support.

(3) Arresting and Constraining Displacement:

Developing countries have little control over product displacement occurring through industrialized country initiatives, especially over industrial production in the North of a crop or product previously exported from the South. There are situations, however, where in-country efforts may be made to contain displacement, especially when it is caused by domestic programs. There also room for cooperation between developing countries and with certain agencies in industrialized countries, as well as with international organizations. Thus, it is possible that through cooperation with universities or small biotechnology companies in the North, as well as through efforts such as the newly established (under UNIDO auspices) International Centre for Genetic Engineering and Biotechnology (ICGEB), developing countries may be able to benefit from biotechnology R and D in an attempt to contain negative impacts.

(4) Identification and Mobilization
     of Affected Interest Groups:

The range of negative impacts caused by product displacement is very broad. However, there are strategies which may be followed in an attempt to lessen some of these impacts. The implementation and success of these strategies depend in large part on the identification of affected parties and on mobilizing them to follow such strategies. The persons and groups who are or will be affected range all the way from producers of agricultural and other raw material products and related industries/services to labor, consumers, and government.

(5) Immediate Action:

In order to implement the strategies outlined above, there is an immediate need for more information on product displacement and its impacts on developing countries. To understand the process of crop/product displacement, it is necessary to explore what is/has been/will be displaced, how displacement occurs, why it occurs, and what time frames are involved in the displacement process.

A first attempt must be made at exploring past instances of displacement to evaluate the interrelations of each of these factors. For example, the R and D process which allowed for displacement of barbasco went on over a period of some twenty years. Yet it was not until Mexico tried to exert some pressure on prices that the product was displaced.

Such analyses should also attempt to determine the
impact that historical instances of displacement have had on
various segments of the population--e.g., farmers and peasants, consumers, labor, business (especially domestic), and
government (through export programs, lost revenues, etc.).

In those instances where policies and programs were
adopted to deal with impacts resulting from displacement--
at any or all of these levels--a review of the impacts and
efficacy of such actions should be made. For example, if,
as in the case of the displacement of sugar in the Philippines, a new product is introduced to help farmers and those
dependent on them to switch to a new crop/product (e.g.,
yellow corn or maize), what impact has this had on such
factors as diets, income, land use, resource use, health,
business related to the two products, exports, government
revenue, other possible crops, or means of livelihood?

These types of case studies would then aid policy-
makers, social action groups, and all others concerned with
those whose current means of subsistence are in danger of
being displaced, in developing early warning systems to
alert the affected parties. This would enable those concerned to draw up strategies for adjustment which would not
only aid in a fairer distribution of the burdens and benefits resulting from the introduction of the technology, but
also avoid switching to programs which themselves are vulnerable to future displacement from new technologies.

IV. INTERNATIONAL DEVELOPMENT AND RURAL IMPOVERISHMENT

INTERNATIONAL DEVELOPMENT AGENCY WORLD VIEWS
ON RURAL DEVELOPMENT: WHO OR WHAT IS CENTRAL?

Reginald Green

International development agency world views of rural
poverty and the rural poor are not homogenous. However, in
both global and national centers (including Third World),
there has been an orthodoxy associated most clearly and lu-
cidly with the World Bank and the UN Food and Agriculture
Organization (FAO). That orthodoxy has been under growing
attack for over a decade from the political and economic
right in the industrialized countries (i.e., Friedmanite/
Reaganite) and from radical critics on the left. The orthodoxy has nonetheless sustained its position so far by incor-
porating much of the market-oriented/"loosers to blame" ideology of the former, while borrowing many of the slogans of
the latter.

This orthodoxy has also borrowed, apparently fleet-
ingly, some of the concerns of its radical critics with the
material needs of the most deprived. To write off the entire McNamara-Chenery-Clark-ul Haq emphasis on absolute
poverty, basic material needs, or the poorest 40 percent as
sloganeering would be both unfair and simplistic. The material welfare of the very poor did come closer to the center
of World Bank concerns (and those of certain major bilateral
programs) and the poor were perceived more as victims and

less as delinquents. However, most of the weaknesses of
the orthodoxy did remain especially the view of the poor as
objects for charity, and of poverty as something to be overcome by managing the poor--a notably "top-down," "paternal-
istic" approach denying the poor any central role in defin-
ing and struggling for their own development.

*Issues of Emphasis and Missing
Links*

The orthodox world view overemphasizes *production* which
it treats as somehow separate from *distribution*. This results in food-demand targets based not on elimination of
hunger but on effective demand (i.e., backed by money to buy
or land to grow food). FAO has consistently adopted this
approach despite verbal bows to its inadequacy, as reflected
in its annual reports over the past decade. India and the
Philippines illustrate that successful programs of this type
(in terms of more production and improved technology) come
up against demand constraints well before supply barriers
and do little or nothing to reduce malnutrition and hunger.

Production and distribution cannot be separated. They
are jointly determined. To accept very unequal access to
land, as well as a rural power structure barring the land-
less/small peasants from effective self-organization to force
up wages (in terms of food purchasable from them), is to
accept their continued exclusion from the right to eat whatever is achieved on the production side. This approach to
rural development is also overly *technocratic*, probably a
result of its heavy emphasis on production and its attempt to
avoid "sensitive" issues of access to earned income and of
power over allocation of resources. In reality, the issues

are only avoided on paper and in analysis since allocation
and distribution continue to take place on the basis of
access and power.

The fact that technical decisions--especially how their
results are delivered to whom--have very real distributional
implications is overlooked or suppressed. For example, in
initial improved maize or corn seed development, the choice
of concentration on strains to be used with high levels of
water and fertilizer inputs was made on technical grounds
without reference to the fact that it excluded the poor
peasants whose land was in dry, non-irrigible areas, and who
could not afford major input costs. This contribution to
increased inequality and absolute impoverishment of some
small peasants was not a matter of ill-will, or conspiracy,
but of a blind faith that technology in practice is value-
free.

Too great an emphasis is placed on *risk taking* within
an overall approach which is overly *economistic*--even "econ-
omystic," where Friedmaniac (or Hayekian) views of the
market as the self-justifying test of equity, democracy, and
efficiency have been incorporated. The poor peasant is a
risk avoider because the margins of survival are slim, major
failure leads to loss of land or life, and the long-run odds
on winning cease to be relevant. The larger the peasant or
landlord and the more dependable his non-agricultural finance
(whether cash reserves or a shop or a salaried position held
by himself or a household member), the more risks are accept-
able. Thus, a risk-oriented strategy is one for increased
polarization, often with the winners gobbling up the losers'
land.

At national or continental levels, the same applies to

food production for domestic consumption versus agricultural
exports. To advocate less emphasis on food production in
low-nutrition, food-importing poor countries by shifting to
export crops (notably, coffee, tea, and cocoa) with uncer-
tain prospects and a record of highly unstable prices is, if
the gamble fails as it very well may, a recipe for rural impoverishment and urban starvation. The inevitable consequences is rising food imports and not enough foreign exchange to pay for them. Yet such a strategy was proposed by
the World Bank in the 1981 report, *Accelerated Development
in Sub-Saharan Africa: An Agenda for Action.*

The economistic bias is seen in the tendency to assume
that sold production is better than household consumption,
that time saved (e.g., by better access to pure water) will
logically all go into production, that women's household
work is not productive, and that popular organization is not
valuable in itself and has a tendency to interfere with
production.

These approaches result in *inadequately articulated* and
unbalanced agendas for action. They seek to develop homogenous checklists for all situations with little real effort
to link analytically grower action principles to specific
cases for action. These action principles are usually in
fact normative, albeit typically asserted as value-free
technical phenomena--for example, that the private sector
is more efficient (for what or whom unspecified) than the
public (World Bank) or that mechanization is the key to increased food production (FAO). The clearest overemphasis is
on general prices, presumably in part because it is easiest
to say somewhat sensible things about them.

Beyond that, long checklists are created to guide

project-level activity. These range from research and extension (hardly ever suggesting their personnel might start by learning what peasants already know) through delivery of inputs on time (much less frequently who actually gets, and doesn't get them and why) to post-harvest losses. These appear quite reasonable, until one looks back and notes that the general checklists and statements of problems of 1980 look remarkably like those of 1960. There is little greater articulation or analysis, and still less evidence (except on improved seed and associated increases in inputs) of much progress on grappling with the underlying problems of access to resources and distribution of power. Even obvious constraints posed by inadequate transport and modern sector storage facilities, central in many African contexts, tend to receive trifling attention, presumably because they do not lend themselves to market-determined ("solved") generalizations.

Food aid appears either as a *deus ex machina* to fill gaps or a supporting input to a technically defined solution (e.g., food for work to create rural infrastructure to support agricultural modernization). It is rarely integrated coherently into any particular rural development strategy, and in particular is not linked to altering access to earned income nor to questions of distribution of land, inputs, and power. The result, predictably, is that it affects these questions in the way that the local power structure favors-- usually but not always (e.g., West Bengal and Kerala in India, formerly Sri Lanka, perhaps Tanzania) in the direction of great inequality and sometimes of pauperization of the small peasantry.

Managing Poverty and the Poor or
Backing Their Struggle Against It?

The international agency world view is highly top down.
This is true even when words like participation by the poor
(in acting on the agenda set for them not by themselves) are
stressed, and genuine human or political insurance or mar-
ket-broadening concerns for reducing poverty are explicitly
and strongly present. This is a logical consequence at the
intellectual level of a production-first, technocracy-in-
command, economistic orientation. Whether it is operational
in its own terms--given its rigidity, limited mass appeal,
and difficulty in relating to specific local conditions--is
an open question. In some cases the answer does seem to be
yes.

There is no intent here to denigrate mutual or overlap-
ping interest arguments as such. Historically, reform has
thrived on a perception that it was necessary to avert ex-
plosions. Civil strife is expensive to the poor, reform can
gain a dynamic of its own and go beyond marginal meliorism.
The poor are bad buyers and payers. If they had access to
earned incomes, they would be better ones.

Even if this is not the central human or moral reason
for seeking to overcome poverty it is one which is not *per
se* immoral, and can--in certain circumstances--gain central
economic decision-taker (state or TNC, capitalist or socialist) support for overcoming poverty. Insisting on final,
pure motives and models--rather than limited, flawed (but
significant) progress, laying the basis for more--is a world
view more associated with not-so-poor intelligentsia than
with actual poor people, including those organized for action
on their own behalf.

But the top-down approach clearly is one in which the poor are objects to be managed, helped to be made less poor, not subjects to be assisted in regaining understanding of, and command over, their own lives in terms and toward goals chosen by them. Combined with an emphasis on neutral technical decisions taken by well-intentioned technocratic experts, this world view totally falsifies reality as it is endured and struggled against by the poor--a contradiction amplified by works such as those by B.B. Schaffer, and by F.F. Piven and R.A. Cloward (see references at end).

The state is thus perceived as a benevolent, detached theraputic agency outside any struggles over power and resources. Technical decisions are seen as eliminating any class or locality or vested-interest conflicts of interest. Political economy is quietly divested both of politics and economics with therapy and technology substituted. In the World Bank annual *World Development Reports*, this attempt produces conundrums. Practices are shown to be oppressive to the poor and dubiously or negatively valid at national economic output level. The question "Why do they continue?" is not put, albeit it is apparently implicitly answered, "Because they hadn't read this report." This is, however intended, pure obfuscation. Most of the practices and policies cited have quite real payoffs for quite real actors with quite real power, and no analysis failing to identify this concretely can form a basis for achieving change.

As political economic theory, this is nonsense in terms of the bourgeois, democratic, pluralist, and orthodox liberal (or for that matter the neo-liberal marketeering) schools of thought as much as the Marxian. It is deeply dangerous because it does not abolish either political

economy or struggle, but merely puts them out of sight where
those who understand them can act with less scrutiny.

Both politicians and technocrats find the model to have
its uses. Overtly, it raises the technocrats' role and
prestige while turning the politicians into benevolent mo-
bilizers for positive, value-free, self-evidently rational
courses of action. When something goes wrong everybody can
avoid the blame: "implementation" was technically unsound,
data were inadequate, the politician didn't understand, the
local elite didn't cooperate, the poor were conservative and
suspicious (as well they may and should be in such context!).
All of these claims may be true but their use in this context is to hide the intellectual fatuity of the model, and
the actual manipulative operational systems to which it provides a spurious cover.

The poor from this point of view *are* victims. Historically, one can admit they have been exploited, excluded,
and oppressed, as long as one does not turn that analysis
into a process which seeks to excuse the continuity in, and
present gainers from, exploitation, exclusion, and oppression. But they are *also* authors and perpetuators of their
own poverty who must either be given safety nets so they
(and the system) survive, or be organized from above to fit
in better and become less poor in ways chosen for and enforced on them.

Toward Alternative World Views

One alternative is the neo-liberal view which fairly
nakedly endorses exploitation and, in principle at least,
concludes that the unexploitable (i.e., "surplus") poor

should be coerced into silence or kept alive if they might otherwise explode. They may be needed as exploitable labor in due course and in the meantime can be tucked into corners of no interest to, and little burden on, the system, otherwise eliminated by whatever method is socially and politically least divisive.

For example, in Bangladesh very poor sub-classes have late marriages, high family break-up rates, and few surviving children because the economic context is such as to make family life and children unsustainable luxuries. The same was true in respect to some sub-classes in 19th-century Ireland (who had, however, the option of emigration as a more human way of removing themselves from being a burden on the system). Literal starvation or mass killing are not the only ways to phase out "superfluous" socio-economic groups.

Neo-liberalism as an intellectual credo is surprisingly widely held in somewhat diluted form, e.g., Henry Kissinger, Mayor Koch, Prime Minister Thatcher. It is an operational force nationally and internationally and its power should not be underemphasized.

Its electoral appeal in functioning capitalist democracies, however, is likely to prove short-lived. There are too many losers who cannot for very long be convinced that their losses are an investment in their own futures. And in the Third World it has tended to be a veneer over much cruder but more locally rooted operational systems of exploitation, domination, and oppression. For example, in Latin America only in Pinochet's Chile can one seriously argue that neo-liberalism may be a co-dominant operational theology. The other national security states and more antiquated juntas have older historic and contextual roots.

If one accepts the Berlinguer (Italian Communist Party) critique of Soviet-model socialism as exemplified in Poland, one might argue that neo-liberalism is likely to find its heartland in industrial socialist politics. However, the differences--turning on the perceptions that the poor are critical as a source of labor power and surplus value and that workers are in short supply/excess supply--mean both less inhumanity at the material level and quite different mechanisms of coercion and management. Admittedly, General Jaruselski's economic policy to date is at certain levels pure state neo-liberalism. But it is based on getting more workers to work harder, not "scrapping" a substantial portion of the population.

In any case, neo-liberalism, while certainly "another" type of development paradigm, can hardly be seen in terms of development of peoples' power or alternatives focused on human need-centered development. Therefore, it will not be considered further here. The fact that it is an extant alternative should, however, give pause to some critics of institutions and individuals backing the orthodox international development asistance model, especially its McNamara variant. There is a real kernel of truth in the classic British nursery warning, "Keep tight hold of nurse for fear of something worse."

The interesting approaches are those development alternatives which are centered on empowerment of the poor as the subjects rather than objects of development. No complete catalogue of contributors to or elements in these approaches is feasible in a brief essay, but several clusters and themes can be identified.

One cluster can be termed unofficial. Among the better

known early examples is *What Now--Another Development,* an
approach followed by the Dag Hammarskjold Foundation, both
with subsequent special volumes and in its journal *Development Dialogue.* Another series is that of the International
Foundation for Development Alternatives (based at Nyon,
Switzerland) but conspicuously trying to reach, and to pub-
lish work by, a fairly extensive global network (admittedly
not one with many poor members). "The Scheveningen Report"
in the 1980/No. 1 issue of *Development Dialogue* is an example of an "unofficial" conceptualization from a mixed global
group of "personalities" acting in their individual capacities.

Another cluster of unofficial alternative approaches to
development has come from religious organizations. Two examples are the monographs of the Advisory Group on Economic
Matters of the World Council of Churches and the series on
Zimbabwe (before independence), Namibia, and South African
liberation and development alternatives published by the
(British) Catholic Institute for International Affairs (in
some cases, jointly with the British Council of Churches).

In a somewhat different position are "unofficial"
approaches. The most important of these is that of the
Brandt Commission. This is a major attempt at reconceptual-
ization, even if its main thrust was programmatic and its
presentation necessarily (given the demi-official charter
and action orientation of the Commission) a bargained com-
promise between global Keynesianism and participatory development propositions. In respect to rural impoverishment and
food, it took a far more radical line than the international
orthodoxy both as to the centrality of overcoming hunger,
and on the need to make structural as well as resource

transfer changes, so that hungry, absolutely poor people (who are largely rural) feed themselves out of their own greater production or earned incomes.

Finally, official international agency concepts and programs have not remained unchanged. The best known single example of formulation is probably the International Labour Office's *Employment, Growth and Basic Needs: A One-World Problem*. It both flowed from employment mission work by the ILO and, following the endorsement of this approach by ILO members, did lead to significant program changes.

It is interesting to read ILO basic needs mission country reports in counterpoint to IMF or World Bank ones. The divergences are substantial, even when there is an overlap in personnel. Perhaps the greatest institutional program shift has been that of the World Health Organization. Its reorientation toward basic health for the poor, paramedical provision of services, and health education and preventative medicine is both far-reaching and very much a break with traditional medical orthodoxy. Two primarily conceptual/modeling-oriented UN agencies have also been active in producing parts of alternatives to internationally orthodox world views. These are the UN Research Institute for Social Development (UNRISD) and the United Nations University. In the food field, the World Food Council has been notably more hunger and poverty-oriented and socio-economic change-focused than FAO and, at least by implication, a severe critic of the former's technocratic, productionist world view.

Processes, Structures, Contexts

The development alternative approaches lay much more
stress on processes, structures, and contexts than does the
orthodox world view. This may make them less general, but
it certainly accords better with the realities of continuity
linked to change and of power exercised though complex social structures (or combatted by organizing counter-struc-
tures). Such emphasis is also likely to fit better with
quite specific needs, constraints, aspirations, and possibilities relating to different historical, material, institutional, and cultural contexts.

For example, hunger is not simply a fact--it is a
reality which is caused and maintained by specific processes
operating with particular internal logics and identifiable
beneficiaries. These processes usually do not aim at producing hunger and may yield substantial benefits to an array
of sub-classes, including some who are poor. A recent World
Council of Churches study of hunger, which made no pretence
at taxonomic completeness, identified seventeen at the national level.

Structures influence outcomes, particularly true of
technological inputs. Who decides what seeds are used for
what purposes (e.g., drought resistance, higher yields with
minimum inputs, disease resistance, nutritional content as
well as, or instead of, maximum yield given a heavy water/
chemical package) heavily conditions who will benefit. Delivery systems for seeds and associated inputs determine to
a large extent who has physical access. Pricing procedures
for seed and other inputs (e.g., private market, free distribution, subsidy, low-selling price clawed back in subsequent purchase prices for crops) condition who can afford to

buy and whose access is effective (e.g., price, membership in bodies given delivery priorities).

Similarly, in respect to technology more generally--both historically and now--both specific institutional and broader socio-economic structures dominate who controls, decides on the uses of, and benefits the most from the technology *per se*. Indeed, these structures heavily condition what knowledge is developed into applied technology and for what uses it is adapted and applied, a proposition closely examined in a World Council of Churches study of transnational corporations, technology, and development.

Contexts are equally critical. For example, to argue that "cows eat people" presupposes a context in which cows eat grain or crops either eaten by people or grown in substitution for human food crops. In Europe and Japan, this presupposition is largely valid. In North America, it is true for perhaps half of beef production. In Asia, Africa, Latin America, and Australasia, it is the exception rather than the rule.

Thus, in Botswana grass-fed cows provide the bulk of rural income and allow significant food purchases in a country which has yet to develop systematic crop production at levels equivalent to self-sufficiency except in years of abnormally favorable rainfall. A case for more emphasis on crop development exists (especially as the poorest rural households are substantially outside the cattle economy), but not because cows eat grain needed by people.

Similarly, to build up animal-drawn implements for agriculture in an area with no previous experience in use of animals for draught power poses complex problems well beyond providing donkeys or oxen and implements. The training and care of the animals, fitting their fodder into production patterns, training peasants in how to use them, identifying and meeting veterinary problems--all are more complex than might be supposed. In the absence of previous experience with animals organized peasant groups require training, advice, and demonstration to make a start.

To argue that poor people can identify their own needs and rights and determine how to organize to achieve them is not to assert that they are technically omniscient. Nor does it mean that they have a broad knowledge of what has proven possible elsewhere and how they could adapt it. Doubtless pure trial and error would provide answers, but at a substantial cost in time and other resources. Such a cost can be justified only by a very dogmatic version of self-reliance and autonomy verging on anarchy and refusal to benefit from the common experience of humanity.

Limitations of Alternative Approaches

These elements or fragments of alternative approaches to rural development suffer from four limitations. First, they tend to be subject to co-optation, especially to the extent that they incorporate elements of non-violent struggle and at least tactical cooperation of the poor with some fractions of the elite. The history of basic human needs as a development focus is a case in point. From its starting point in the Dag Hammarskjold Foundation's *What Now* to its maximum official formulation in the ILO's *Employment Growth and Basic Needs: A One-World Problem*, it has since descended to a quarrying ground for bits and pieces of basic material need programs, abstracted from both meaningful participation and struggle.

Second, some variants, notably those of basically authoritarian Western authors like Johan Galtung and Dieter Senghaas and of technocratically manned bodies like UNRISD and the UN University, mount quite astoundingly complex conceptualization, examination, and analysis models. Apart from the danger of technicism run mad, these are a form of "black boxing" (Western witchcraft?), which prevents them from being understood and controlled by the poor and makes them likely to end as part of the problem, not of the answer.

Third, there is a tendency to slide into conspiracy theories and/or counter-simplification. Technology is not itself a conspiracy nor is its use necessarily so. Transnational corporations pursue growth, accumulation, profit, survival, power, and production within a logic which is more amoral (and thus subject to being used for immoral ends) and unaccountable (and therefore likely to exclude human beings most affected from consideration) than it is purposefully evil. The justified moral outrage of some writers--for example, Susan George in *How the Other Half Dies*--at the amorality leading to immoral results under the cover of technically determined, value-free public image models creates another kind of danger. That danger involves slipping into a perception of reality as a conspiracy rather than as a process of struggle. This is dangerous because it clouds analysis, especially of how holders of power (e.g., TNCs) might actually be constrained to act differently.

Similarly, rejecting the somewhat unfocused use of food aid as a means of subsidizing Northern farmers can be asserted as a way to help the poor and/or the development of the Third World. But it does not lead logically to

denunciation of balance of payments support transfers to
food-deficit countries made in food, nor to the concept of
linking food allocations (globally or nationally) to rural
development strategies. To end all food transfers now without doing anything else on the production or distribution
side would be a recipe for starvation. To the extent that
certain writers--for example, Tony Jackson writing for Oxfam
or C. Fryer writing for a World Council of Churches project--
advocate that, they are even less clear-sighted or humanly
responsible than the international orthodoxy. (Neither
Oxfam nor the World Council of Churches accepts this simplified approach in practice, and possibly neither would the
authors if they actually felt their writings could lead to
a sudden cutoff of food transfers.)

Fourth, these fragments are just that. When embodied
in particular alternative developments they are a kind of
inversion of the orthodoxy, too particular and context-bound
to make identification of their general principles fully
possible. At the more global level, they tend either to be
logical sets of conceptual boxes, which unfortunately lack
concrete objective correlatives to fit into many of the
boxes, or to be a set of guidelines and norms which are
neither rigorously enough argued, nor articulated coherently
enough to grassroots applications, to constitute a genuine
paradigm. Both the human rights versions of basic human
needs and the World Council of Churches "Just, Participatory
and Sustainable Society" formulation are very much open to
these criticisms.

162

Legal Resources: Potential Parts
of Solutions

Legally trained personnel are not normally regular
members of peoples' movements, nor of the organized (or unorganized) poor. Therefore, even when genuinely in solidarity with them, they cannot provide leadership, blueprints, institutional structures, or alternative technical
answers without falling back into the orthodox international development assistance model criticized above.

However, this should not be read as arguing either that
there is no role for legal resources in development alternatives, or that legally trained personnel should be totally
passive responders to specific requests from the organized
poor. That approach is too narrow for at least three
reasons.

First, the organized poor do need to deal with loci of
power and with elites, usually by means other than naked
confrontation. Therefore, they require persons who can interpret power centers and their applicable logic as well as
their rights, needs, programs, and claims to power centers.

Second, to argue that self-liberation and consciousness-
raising are key, and outside leadership often as obstacle,
is quite consistent with believing that genuinely supportive
"outsiders" with knowledge and expertise can act both as input providers and catalysts. This is especially so if the
outsiders have the humility not to try to dominate or to
turn initial "stimulatory leadership" roles into permanent
institutional ones.

Third, peoples' organizations have quite specific needs
for legal inputs. These include defending their members and
structures, identifying ways of using existing legal systems,

and formulating proposals for attainable and functional
legal system changes (either to protect gains initially won
by nonlegal means, or to highlight contradictions between
"agreed" norms and actual practice). Other legal inputs
involve developing their own institutions' "constitutional
and administrative law" and "dispute settlement" structures,
negotiating with outside power foci, and training their own
members in paralegal and specific legal skills.

This suggests a complex role for legally trained
personnel--one with several aspects not all of which are
likely to be carried on regularly by any one individual.
One cluster consists of fairly standard legal services--
defending clients, formulating cases for them, advising on
avoiding litigation, and negotiating settlements. A second
is "promotional"--showing how such organizations have worked,
when, and why with a view to furthering their success. A
third is analytical and conceptual but with the aim of providing inputs in a form which groups of the organized rural
poor can understand, master, and use for themselves. A
fourth is *ad hoc* legal and paralegal education. A final
cluster is that of catalytic and supportive technical leadership.

Knowledge can be power and acquiring self-knowledge is
a process which can benefit, especially in its early stages,
from outside questions and comments. But this is true only
so long as these questions and comments do not degenerate
into overbearing rhetoric unrelated to the immediate context
or become a procrustean agenda that reflects the priorities
of the outsiders and not the people themselves.

164

References

Brandt Commission, *North-South: A Program for Survival,* Cambridge, MA: MIT Press, 1980.

Dag Hammarskjold Foundation, "Towards a New International Development Strategy," *Development Dialogue,* No. 1, 1980.

Dag Hammarskjold Foundation, *What Now--Another Development,* Uppsala: The Foundation, 1975.

Asbjorn Eide *et al, Food as a Human Right,* Tokyo: United Nations University, 1984.

S. George, *How the Other Half Dies,* London: Pelican, 1976.

R.H. Green, "Brandt on an End to Poverty and Hunger," *Third World Quarterly,* Vol. 3, No. 1, January 1981.

International Foundation for Development Alternatives, *IFDA Dossier,* Nyon, Switzerland: IFDA, bimonthly.

International Labour Office, *Employment, Growth and Basic Needs: A One-World Problem,* Geneva: ILO, 1976.

A.H. Jamal, "Man at the Centre of Economic Purpose," *Third World Quarterly,* Vol. 3, No. 1, January 1981.

F.F. Piven and R.A. Cloward, *Regulating the Poor: The Function of Public Welfare,* New York: Vintage, 1972, especially chapter 9 on "The Great Society and Relief."

B.B. Schaffer, "To Recapture Public Policy for Politics," *Politics, Administration and Change,* VII:1, January-June, 1982.

J. Schatan, "A Project Illustration: Concepts and Methods in 'Food Systems and Society'," Oslo Workshop on "Food as a Human Right," September 1981 (on the UN Research Institute for Social Development Food Systems Project).

World Bank, *Accelerated Development in Sub-Saharan Africa: An Agenda for Action,* Washington, D.C.: The Bank, 1981.

World Bank, *World Development Report*, Washington, D.C.: The Bank, annual.

World Council of Churches, Commission on Churches' Participation in Development, *Ecumenism and a New World Order*, Geneva: The Council, 1980; *Transnational Corporations, Technology and Human Development*, Geneva: The Council, 1981; *Hunger of Justice and Bread for the Hungry*, Geneva: The Council, 1982.

INTERNATIONAL DEVELOPMENT ASSISTANCE:

AUTHORITARIAN NON-ACCOUNTABILITY

Reginald Green

The administrative and decision-taking approach of international development assistance--whether intentionally or otherwise--is dominated by a vision of platonic guardian-ship, top-down authoritarianism, bureaucratic manipulation, and upward accountability. In a sense these represent a continuity with colonialism, notwithstanding the much more prominent tendency to "de-politicize" public policy (by masking ideology in supposedly value-free expertise) than in colonial pronouncements or practice. Also new (or neo-colonial) is a repetitive tendency to create parallel insti-tutional structures responsible to the external aid agency, but bypassing both local peoples and national (whether elite or popular) channels and structures.

The central issue is not whether international resource-transferring bodies mean well. Nor is it whether their ad-vice is sound. Even if both questions can be answered in the affirmative (sometimes, though by no means always the case), the attempted depoliticization of public policy, the granting of unchecked power to experts and elites cooper-ating with them, and the deliberate confusion of technical facts with what are necessarily value judgments--all are deeply inimical to peoples' organizations, popular participation, and development. (This critique has been expounded in a recent paper by B.B. Schaffer; see references at end of this essay.)

External Organizations and Experts Know Best

International resource transfer agencies rarely admit past mistakes and almost always assert clarity, applicability, and correctness for their present view. They show very little sense of humility and uncertainty. The variety of experiences and contexts with which they must deal make universal export policy models highly unsuitable for general, unadapted use. These characteristics are not altered by experience. Past advice followed by the recipient to his disadvantage (or benefit, as the case may be) is cited as his mistake if the agency or expert has now changed its or his interpretation.

Particular examples and broad principles are often cited. What is usually absent is any articulation between them. The examples can be fitted into alternative interpretations and proposals, each of which may be appropriate at some time and place. The broad principles flow from value judgments, such as the market knows best or local decisions and knowledge are always faulty (except apparently those of international aid experts)! They also flow from Western intellectual styles, e.g., the bowdlerized "basic material needs" approach of the late 1970s which sounded more like a plan for the care and rearing of dairy cattle than an approach to meeting essential human needs.

It is invidious to cite examples since few international development agencies, whether bilateral or multilateral, can

escape these criticisms. But no better illustration can be
found than the present World Bank approach to sub-Saharan
Africa as exemplified in the "Berg report" of 1981. This is
especially true of its views that more coffee, tea, and
cocoa and less food should be grown, and that parallel institutions responsible to the World Bank bypassing basic
national structures are wrong. The first of these almost
certainly is hopelessly unsound--both technically and dis-
tributionally. The second is probably politically and
functionally sound in most contexts if one favors local and
peoples' control over their own affairs and welfare. However, the validity of present stands is not the point at
issue here. Each of these is a totally unacknowledged reversal of policy as is the downgrading of health, education,
and low-income group welfare in the overall strategic proposals (although not in the chapters actually dealing with
the health and education sectors).

There are exceptions to this pattern. For example, the
World Health Organization, UNICEF (the UN Children's Fund),
and, in part, the International Labour Office are examples
among multilateral official agencies and the Nordic among bilateral aid agencies. (There is great unevenness by section
and program in the ILO. The core ILO activities before it
broadened its approach to workers and to development are much
more in the standard, platonic guardianship pattern.) But
these remain embattled exceptions under pressure to conform,
as do individual experts who disagree with the cult of the
foreign expert which they find morally obnoxious and opera-
tionally counter-productive to the supposed beneficiaries.
As with poverty so with development. It is much more profitable to be an expert analyst and prescribe about it however

often the prescriptions go disastrously wrong and however shoddy the analysis, than to be a poor person who actually works successfully at overcoming personal, family, and community poverty by achieving development.

Platonic Guardianship and Bureaucratic Process

Externally based expertise normally operates via dependent local bureaucracies, client local elites, and manipulated workers and peasants. Its appeals are to commandism, hierarchy, and "value-free" technocracy insulated from political accountability. Its relationships are with the local "big battalions" which are easiest for external "big battalions" to relate to, and with local (almost always elite) individuals who share or appear to share its technical and cultural world view.

Because technocrats know best, there is no need to learn from local experience (except perhaps that of other experts) and especially not from workers and peasants. As a result, a command structure to enforce acceptance of expert prescriptions and expert-identified resource deliveries appears to be efficient. It is backed by education--of workers and villages to obey, and of low-level cadres to "manage" workers and villages on the basis of these prescriptions handed down by experts.

The ILO's "module" training program is an urban and agribusiness example (at least if it is viewed, as the ILO asserts it should be, as more than a simplified on-the-job approach to upgrading to semi-skilled and semi-artisan positions). The World Bank's proposed conversion of Tanzanian village managers from village-selected, village member cadres (who learn technical skills under the direction of village councils) into secondary school leaders trained to manage (i.e., direct) villagers and village councils is an even more telling example. Luckily few villages in Tanzania have been inert or inept enough to accept this imposition. As a result, most managers manage only their own paperwork. Some have accepted roles of serving villages within terms of reference set by them and a not insignificant number have been rejected by villages and forced out by their pressure.

Needless to say this approach is not, in principle, unacceptable to local experts and officials who fit fairly well into its lower and middle cadres. If they accept it fully, however, they become more and more dependent on the external agency's local control group. For example, the World Bank/FAO-sponsored and dominated Marketing Development Bureau (MDB) in Tanzania systematically arrogates all key technical and policy advising functions to itself and takes care to prevent the emergence of domestic competitors.

A similar tendency arises in choice of cooperating institutions. The international resource transfer agencies are bureaucratic "big battalions." They relate easily to their counterparts abroad and very uneasily to overtly political (especially populist or radical) bodies and ill-defined, small peoples' organizations. This can lead to remarkable defensiveness by such agencies toward self-evidently, over-centralized, and badly functioning large bureaucratic bodies when they are under domestic attack for exploitation, loss of funds, or sheer physical incompetence--for example, the MDB's protection of Tanzania's National Milling Corporation floated in 1974 largely on the advice of USAID experts.

The symbiotic relationships between international and

local experts and between external and domestic big battalions uniformly reinforce hierarchicalism and commandism.
They cannot be said to have any similarly uniform positive
impact on quantity, quality, or cost of production. Their
impact on genuine local initiative, self-reliance, and
accountability is normally highly negative.

Who Responds? How?

Technocratic, top-down approaches do cause responses,
at least if they are backed by sufficient carrots (resources
to be awarded to clients) and sticks (coercion, isolation,
and exclusion from benefits of those who do not "cooperate"
or "participate"). One of the most unfortunate aspects of
this kind of approach is its tendency to cloak itself in the
verbiage of cooperation and participation while using an ideological and operational approach quite antithetical to them.
Oddly, many practitioners can see this shortcoming in other
experts and institutions, but quite genuinely fail to per-
ceive it in themselves. In extreme cases, such experts speak
of "saving" peasants not merely from their states and large
(public or private) corporations, but also from village councils and economic organizations created, operated, and controlled by them.

The critical questions are who responds and how. Any
quick answers are oversimplified; patterns vary widely in
detail.

"Progressive farmers" respond and collect the carrots.
Progressive in this context usually means above average in
income with access to resources and contacts in the official
and elitist sectors--farmers who are somewhat more educated
and (at least apparently) culturally attuned to the experts.

Linked to them are officials with similar characteristics. The problem is not that these individuals are evil, but that they are atypical--*asomi* in the semi-admiring, semi-perjorative East African term for the semi-modernized, semi-Westernized, upwardly mobile African who is largely detached from his own community.

The international agency approach produces inequality and divisiveness because of the sub-class specificity of respondents and beneficiaries. It is even more deeply divisive because it pulls *asomi* away from their communities and bases, thereby robbing peoples' organizations of many who might, in different contexts, work as leaders and experts within these organizations.

For others the response is "positive" because of the stick. Manipulation assures their participation not because they are better off but because refusal to cooperate bears a higher price. Many rural development schemes--for example, those of the Fleuve province of Senegal and of the "pseudo cooperative" palm oil plantations of Sumatra--are glaring examples.

Finally, many respond by "retreat," escaping from the formal economy into subsistence agriculture and small-scale urban crafts and services. This option may prevent damage to peasant and worker well-being--the isolated Casamance Province of Senegal seems to be an example--but it does prevent, by self-isolation, the acquisition of external contacts and inputs usually needed to start even a locally based, self-reliant process of development.

One-Way Accountability

International development agencies do not lack a
concept of accountability. The problem is that it is from
the bottom up--to themselves--and effectively renders them
totally non-accountable to the supposed intended beneficiaries.

In the standard rural development model, peasants are
to be accountable to technical agricultural officers and to
village and co-op managers. These are, in turn, accountable
to higher levels of technocrats who are ultimately responsible to the aid agency and, if this cannot be avoided, to
national political decision-takers. If possible, the national accountability should be minimized by parallel
structures and enclave programs.

In fairness, the problems of operating in a context of
elite corruption or oppression which often confront these
agencies do create real pressures to adopt this course. If
it were linked to accepting effective accountability to
actual workers and peasants, a moral case might be made for
it. However, even then one may query the plausibility of the
World Bank mobilizing peasants to assert their rights against
the host state or the practical potential of the Swedish-
protected rural enclaves created by SIDA's rural development
effort in late imperial Ethiopia.

From the political point of view this is not accountability; rather it is a denial of accountability. These
arrangements frustrate development of domestic political
accountability. They lead to growing agency/host government
tensions (especially if political accountability to workers
and peasants is to some extent a reality), and they hamper
peoples' organizational efforts to mobilize and to control

those who affect their members' lives.

Legal Resources, Mobilization,
and Accountability

Legal resources can be relevant to building structures
of popular participation and accountability to constrain and
perhaps change the impact of international aid agencies.
The starting premises are three:

a) No viable development can be achieved through
    bypassing local institutions and accountabil-
    ity as opposed to strengthening them.

b) Public policy must be recaptured for politics
    and accountability, not left to the hidden
    value judgments of non-accountable technocrats
    and elites.

c) Popular organizations--e.g., of workers,
    peasants, women, consumers, ethnic and caste
    minorities--can be effective as political
    pressure groups and so direct self-reliant de-
    velopment foci. Thus, their mobilization and
    strengthening is critical to realizing the
    right to development.

Legally trained personnel can be of value in providing
information on existing legal structures and opportunities
and on advising in respect to negotiations. They can also
point out both formal legal and direct political pressure
means to begin enforcing accountability on local landlords
and traders, local-level state officers, higher state bureaucracies and institutions, and ultimately, through national institutions, on international development agencies.

In addition, because legally trained personnel do speak
the language of international experts, they may be able to
act in solidarity with peoples' organizations by interpreting

them to international experts. WHO's conversion to rural, people-based health programs and the ILO's adoption of Convention 141--covering the rights of rural workers (including small peasants) to organize and to act on a self-help basis-- demonstrate that international organizations can respond to popular aspirations and pressures and act to affirm their rights. In both cases, experts (as it happens not legally trained experts) who stood in solidarity and close contact with the people directly affected played crucial roles in achieving these altered development world views and operational priorities.

References

B.B. Schaffer, "To Recapture Public Policy for Politics," *Politics, Administration and Change*, VII:1, January-June, 1982.

World Bank, *Accelerated Development in Sub-Saharan Africa: An Agenda for Action* ("Berg Report"), Washington, D.C.: The Bank, 1981.

BUILDING EXPORT MARKETS FOR THE FIRST WORLD THROUGH
"DEVELOPMENT": THE CASE OF OPERATION FLOOD IN INDIA

Claude Alvares

Another Revolution Fails

India's dairy project, Operation Flood, is often touted
as the largest development program of its kind in the Third
World.[1] Based on gifted dairy commodities from the EEC and
directed by two public sector organizations in India--the
National Dairy Development Board (NDDB) and the Indian Dairy
Corporation (IDC)[2]--Operation Flood has also been sold to a
global public as a major success in cooperative enterprise,
enabling a majority Third World interest group (namely,
farmers) to get a better price for their milk, not only
through better markets in the cities but also via a more so-
phisticated product mix of dairy products, including cheese
and chocolates (whose production was once the preserve of
transnationals).

Operation Flood is based on food aid in a new form.
Surplus milk powder and butter oil from the EEC's "fabled
mountains" of such commodities are shipped to India's IDC and
then sold by the IDC to the metropolitan dairies, who recon-
stitute it into fluid milk and other dairy products for sale
to the general public. The funds generated through the sale
are used to enhance the modernization of the dairy sector and
of the people involved in the trade. Funds are also set

aside to form "Anand"-type[3] milk cooperatives in different parts of the country, which are meant not only to give their members a fair price for their milk but also access to modern inputs to further increase milk production.

In the cities, in the meanwhile, consumers are provided with quality-controlled milk and milk products according to their consumer preferences, which may include either Western-style items like cheese, baby food, or chocolates, or such Indian-style items as *ghee* or *shrikhand*.[4] Eventually, as a result of efforts to provide better markets and to directly improve milk production, it is hoped that the indigenous production of fresh milk would dramatically improve, thus enabling the modern dairies to end their reliance on imported milk powder by the time the project officially ends in mid-1985.

This form of food aid is seen by its adherents as aid that is mutually beneficial to the interests of both donor and receiving countries. The receiving country has access to a massive source of funds that would never be available in the country itself in the normal course. And the fact that the aid is not given free *within* the economy of the developing country could also presumably help it avoid the crippling effects on local production that previous programs, including the PL-480 aid program, obviously had. Further, it also enables the ruling political elite to conveniently lavish scarce public revenues generated within the country on such fashionable projects as nuclear weapons, nuclear power, and space technology.

For the EEC, food aid is a convenient option for getting rid of embarrassing surpluses that need no longer be sold to politically distasteful countries like the Soviet Union.

More importantly, food aid provides the easiest possible, legitimate channel for creating long-term markets for dairy commodities in the Third World. The reputed success of Operation Flood in India has now resulted in its propagation to other countries, including the Philippines, Sri Lanka, Bangladesh, Pakistan, and China.

An almost classic description of the advantages of such food aid for the *donor* countries was given involuntarily by Verghese Kurien himself in an interview with a Bombay magazine in March 1984. Said Kurien:

> In the first paper the Dairy Board of India submitted to the government (of India), we had said that some kindly old gentleman is going to turn up one morning from Europe and he is going to tell our Honorable Minister, "Look, your people are starving. What they need is milk. I will *give* it to you." I went on to argue in this note that any gift of commodities, say of 100 million dollars, is in reality an *investment* of 100 million in our country by this foreign aid agency. They give us this aid because they have a surplus. They give us the aid because they have to maintain their farmers' prices. They give us this aid because they cannot sell their produce. Once they have given it to us, that will create residual demand. You can't have a child-feeding program and shut it off tomorrow because the powder stopped coming. So there will be a residual demand and even with our best efforts that demand will be at least 10 percent which means that the return on the investment of 100 million dollars is 10 million dollars per year. But if, in the process of giving us this aid, they have liquidated their surpluses, the prices will be restored to normalcy. That would double the price, let us say. Therefore, to buy that 10 percent, we will have to pay double! So food aid must be looked upon, I wrote in this note, as an *investment* being made in our country.[5]

An all-win development project: consumers in Indian cities are to be provided with fresh quality milk, and the country is to attain self-sufficiency in dairy products by the time the project ends; farmers are to get a better price and infrastructural support for their labor; and a preferred development model based on cooperatives is to be given major support and political space. The EEC, in the process, gets rid of unwanted surplus stocks, and also achieves a reputation for generosity and concern for the needy. On paper, a seemingly ideal project, and to be therefore wholeheartedly supported and strengthened.

What went wrong?

When a development project goes off the rails it invariably also ends up as a destructive monstrosity. This has happened time and again. Development projects designed to ameliorate, to emancipate, have led to increased impoverishment, greater social disparities, and even more deeply entrenched vested interests.

There have been any number of glorious revolutions in the Third World, all of them initiated by the establishment. We know the fate of the Green Revolution. India today has stored stocks of 22 million tons of grain, but half the population continues to suffer grossly inadequate diets. The almost exclusive investment of most development funds in a few regions like the Punjab and Haryana has led to the further erosion of traditional agriculture in the rest of the country. The same experience has dogged the Blue Revolution. Previously, entire coastal populations enjoyed relatively easy access to fish protein. This is no longer the case, as the fish now ends up in Tokyo and Paris and traditional fishermen have been left in ruins. The White Revolution (dairying) carries its own perverse tale. It is instructive to examine its history, its divergence from professed goals and objectives, and to see how it has led to the impoverishment of large masses of people in the country.

In fact, more than the Green Revolution, it is the White Revolution that has signaled the most radical form of intervention of Western technology in such a core sector as Indian dairying. Since the predominant ideal has been to ape the West, the entire development strategy for milk production and distribution has closely paralleled the experience of the West. Not only do the base stocks of Skim Milk Powder (SMP) and Butter Oil (BO) originate from the EEC; the dairy equipment has also come basically from European transnationals. A small piece of Holland or Denmark has been carved out in India, with even cattle breeds imported from such countries. The only Indian factor has been the farmer!

In order to force dramatic short-term gains, the White Revolution has compromised the long-term survival of the dairy system, and also considerably weakened the coping abilities of the rest of the population. Operation Flood is a clear instance of how a major business operation of cooperative capitalism has been passed off as a developmental transformation. It has brought a traditionally accessible and essential commodity like milk into the realm of economic scarcity, and dramatically increased the availability of milk and milk products for the upper classes at the cost of reducing consumption of the essential protein among rural populations.

India's Traditional Dairying System

Two preliminary points need to be made concerning the subject of dairying in India. The first is that dairying by itself can never become a principal occupation of farmers in India, simply because the cattle economy is primarily directed toward the needs of agriculture, and the production of milk is a secondary, almost unintended, business. Even the fodders available to animal stock consist basically of sources of food not consumed by humans. Agricultural wastes and browsing over common lands and in forests constitute an almost free resource.

The second point concerns the inclusion of milk in diets. India has primarily a vegetarian population, and for this vast group of people the only source of first-class animal protein is milk and milk products. Surprisingly, the poorest economic groups themselves traditionally have access to other sources of protein. The outcastes, for example, have relied on meat, and the tribals on game and other unconventional sources like insects, while coastal areas have relied on fish. But for those with no such access, Indian society traditionally has provided access to milk in processed form. For example, of all the milk produced, the largest quantity goes for the production of ghee (in the production of which buttermilk becomes available and which was never sold, but distributed freely in the village). There has also been a bewildering variety of sweets made from milk, in addition, of course, to milk being consumed directly or used in such beverages as tea.

Thus, Indian civilization over centuries has gradually perfected a system which enabled large numbers of animals to be maintained to produce some milk as an important by-product, of a strategy to maintain primarily draught power using waste materials and fodders, as well as involving a subsidiary rural occupation in the production of butter and ghee. Of course, due to such pressures as population increase, but primarily because of the increasing concentration of what were earlier common resources in the hands of aggrandizing ruling classes, the system was showing signs of exhaustion, already manifest in the form of overgrazing of pasture lands, decline in the productivity of indigenous breeds, and so forth.

This has been recognized and a number of government-patronized programs had been initiated to reverse the imbalance. The problem of supplying milk for urban requirements was also acute, but it was temporarily resolved by relying on relatively cheap SMP imports from abroad and on cattle colonies within city limits. Most government milk programs concentrated on increasing the quantity of milk _and_ its consumption in the rural areas. Planning documents clearly state that only the surplus milk from the rural areas must be taken to the nearest towns and, thereafter, to the cities. Government efforts to increase milk production initially relied almost exclusively on selective breeding of indigenous stock. Later, the policy was abruptly changed to one of crossbreeding with exotic breeds from Europe and America. Although it was recognized that the crossbred bulls that would result were more or less useless as draught power, this was not then seen as a problem because planners had already decided in favor of tractorization of field operations.

*The Kaira District Cooperative Milk
Producer's Union*

The Kaira (Kheda) district in Gujarat, with its headquarters at Anand, was no exception to the general rule.
But dairying here had had a long-standing history going back
to 1900 and earlier. In 1945, when local politicians decided to use cooperatives as a new form of reorganizing
their political bases, they found Kaira farmers fit material
for trying out the idea. The number of cooperatives rapidly
increased, partly because as cooperatives they were soon
able to use central government clout to corner milk supply
contracts to the city of Bombay, 200 miles away to the south.
Mr. Verghese Kurien joined the Kaira District Cooperative
Milk Producer's Union in 1950, five years after the Cooperative was formed. He did not begin cooperative farming in
the area: that was a singular contribution of the farmers
themselves on the inspiration of their political leaders.

The immediate problem the Kaira Union faced concerned
the surplus milk available in the "flush" season. (In India,
milk production is still "flush" after the rains due to good
fodder and seasonal calving, with the "lean" season ranging
from April to August.) The solution was a milk powder plant,
which enabled them to process the surplus, and thus equipped
them to purchase all the milk available without any further
difficulty, providing further incentive for milk production.
The Union then sought to diversify its product mix into baby
food, condensed milk, and cheese. Seventy-five percent of
its growth was already established prior to 1970, the year in
which Operation Flood was launched. The Kaira Union is today
one of India's top 30 companies in terms of profits, and one
of the most successful examples of cooperative capitalism

anywhere in the world. In the late 1960s, it was India's largest producer of butter and milk powder and dominated the market entirely through Amul products, the registered brand name of the Kaira Union. At this time, however, Europe's dairy industry had begun to accumulate phenomenal surpluses of precisely these two commodities--milk powder and butter. Once the news spread that these stocks would soon be gifted to such countries as India, Amul officials began to take notice. A free consignment of 20,000 tons of milk powder and just 10,000 tons of butter would wipe out the commercial successes of Amul, painstakingly achieved over a period of 20 years.

The initiative for Operation Flood, therefore, came not from the Government of India or from the EEC, but from Verghese Kurien and his close associates in Amul. Amul itself required little development aid to start its dairy, modernize it, or form more cooperatives; it already was a successful enterprise. But if Amul could propose a development project involving free European supplies, which it would control and direct (and thus safeguard its own commercial success), this would be far better than leaving such important developments as EEC aid merely to chance--or to the whim of politicians who might use them for their own short-term goals (e.g., keeping prices down below that dictated by the market).

National Dairy Development Board/
Indian Dairy Corporation

Amul employees fought for and obtained total control of the project. The National Dairy Development Board (NDDB), formed in 1965, had a number of Amul employees on its board of directors, and its chairman has been none other than Verghese Kurien. But as a society, the NDDB could not under existing laws take on a project like Operation Flood which involved the business of selling commodities. Hence, the Government of India was advised to set up the Indian Dairy Corporation in 1970, of which Verghese Kurien was again made chairman. During the period that he occupied both these posts in the public sector, he insisted on continuing his employment with the Amul Cooperative as chairman and managing director. Thus, effective control of the Operation Flood project would remain always in Anand. The Government of India then proceeded to wipe its hands of the project. Operation Flood I (1970-1981) was outside the Plan budget. Although Operation Flood II (1978-1985) was brought within the Plan budget, no ministerial power was made available to check matters if they went awry.

As a consequence, the NDDB/IDC moved with a vengeance to erode the entire edifice of the animal husbandry divisions of the central and state governments--manned as they were by "bureaucrats" for whom Kurien had scant respect and constituting a parallel source of authority. Operation Flood received the major portion of funds for dairy development, including the upgrading of livestock and other projects such as the propagation of fodder farms. Effective control remained with the NDDB, which has until now maintained its audits outside the purview of the Auditor and Comptroller General of India.

Such a situation has never occurred before on such a scale. In the Green Revolution, the IARI and the ICAR remained the main agents for propagation and control. In the case of the White Revolution, government personnel were gradually eclipsed in favor of a private group hardly accountable to the public. Kurien himself, although he remained chairman of IDC/NDDB, never became a government servant by drawing his statutory salary of Rs. 1 from the two organizations. In the end, it was he who formulated dairy policy, and whenever any major policy deviations were announced he could always claim that it was government that had made the new policy (at the same time not disclosing that he constituted the government in such matters).

The central Indian Government itself kept changing during these critical years. When the project began, the Congress was in power. In 1977, the Janata came to power, led by Morarji Desai who had been involved in the formation of the Kaira Union in 1945. And in 1980, Mrs. Gandhi returned with the Congress. No evaluation was ever made of the project, although one proposed during Janata rule was scuttled by the intervention of Kurien.

Yet, despite these changes at the center, the commitment of the Indian Government to Anand was constant. In fact, even today Anand offers Delhi a glamor project for international visitors who wish to see some development successes. What is not realized is that the cooperative movement was a creation of local farmers and their political leaders. Further, the glamor had been enhanced by Amul's ability to bring in handsome grants from development organizations, including such agencies as Oxfam and UNICEF. The fact that it is one of the top 30 companies in India in terms of profits still did not prevent it from masquerading as an institution in need of charity. Anand is today an essential stop in development tourism, just as the Jamkhed project in Maharashtra has become the mecca for all medical projects.

It is also part of the nature of such projects that
they encourage a largely adulatory press: at one time or
another, most of India's leading newspapermen have been in-
vited to Anand, given lavish hospitality, and thus been
subtly influenced in favor of the project. But such uncrit-
ical roles have not been restricted to the press alone. So-
called evaluation teams consisting of dairy specialists and
technicians have also willingly played the politics of the
media and defended the project against unfavorable images.
For example, after a whirlwind study the UN terminal evaluation team (headed by Henryk Jasiorowski, rector of Warsaw
Agricultural University in Poland) immediately held a press
conference, even before its report[6] had been written and
submitted to the relevant authorities, in an effort to im-
press upon journalists that criticism of the project was
unfounded.

Operation Flood: Well-Intentioned
or Misconceived?

The word "Operation" in the name Operation Flood de-
rives from cheap James Bond movies of yesteryear, in which
spies operated against spies and programs were executed in
secret chambers to produce subversive results. The word has
now become part of establishment terminology and it ideally
describes how technocrats or militia in Third World countries *execute* projects in which people are targets. Operation Flood promised to "flood" the country with milk. And
the White Revolution imagery was used to imply that a major
socioeconomic transformation was underway in farmers' lives
because of the project's efforts.

Operation Flood was based on five operating principles:

(1) The EEC would convert its butter into butter oil and this, together with SMP (Skim Milk Powder), would be recombined into fluid milk and used to "prime the pump," so to say, for the four metro dairies of Calcutta, Madras, Bombay, and Delhi. The milk would be sold at prices high enough to prevent their acting as a depressant on indigenous production.

(2) The funds thus generated would be used for project investments, increasing the capacity of the metro dairies so that they could meet increasing demand.

(3) Once the metro dairies captured a commanding share of their city markets, cattle colonies in these areas would be forced back into rural areas, where milk production would be more economic. This would also prevent the slaughter and drain of genetic stock, as evident in current city dairy practice. The funds would also be used to set up milk cooperatives on the Anand pattern, and upon the project's termination these cooperatives would supply all the milk required by the dairies, thus enabling dependence on imported milk powder and butter oil.

(4) Thus, the better breeds and high-yielding animals would remain in the rural areas, where funds would be used to provide the technical inputs for improving stock so that the continuous improvement of stock would enable a steady increase in milk production into the future.

(5) Since the country's milk production still relied on monsoon rains, and drought was an unpredictable but constant factor, it was anticipated that some regions might suffer milk production deficits. As a consequence, a national milk grid was planned that would help even out

year-to-year seasonal and regional imbalances.

The agreement signed in March 1970 between the World
Food Programme and the Government of India (Project India
618) also made a number of specific demands. The agreement
stipulated as one of its objectives making "available whole-
some milk at stable and reasonable prices to the bulk of
city consumers, including vulnerable groups, namely pre-
school children, nursing and expectant mothers, etc., with
major effects on protein intake."[7] And it committed government to produce special reconstituted milk in each of the
four cities with 1.5 percent fat and 9 percent nonfat solids
to meet the needs of such vulnerable groups as infants,
children, expectant and nursing mothers, and the lower-
income sections of the population. In addition, the World
Food Programme agreed to undertake, among other things,
studies on the impact of the food aid on the improvenent of
the nutritional status and the economic and social development of the country on a long-term basis.

Eventually, these specific directives concerning socio-
economic objectives were thrown to the winds, thus bringing
into question the involvement of the Government of India in
the project via such public sector corporations as the IDC
and NDDB, and also, as far as European citizens were concerned, the rationale of giving food aid. It transpired
later that being businessmen, project officials did not
really believe in any direct efforts to improve milk productivity. Instead, they felt that once a good market was provided, milk production would automatically increase. "I
shall put my buck where I can get the best bang out of it,"
said R.P. Aneja, Secretary to the NDDB. The strategy was to
construct milk collection and chilling plants (whether there

was sufficient milk in the area or not) in order to thus
stimulate farmers to go in for more milk production. Soon
milk marketing overtook milk production and the strategy refused to work. When the first project came to a close in
1981, despite a six-year extension the country was as dependent as ever on imported milk powder and butter oil.

In the meanwhile, the Amul cooperative made good the
opportunity to exploit the project to expand its own production base. Credits and grants were easily available and the
person to sanction it all was also an employee. Thus, despite the fact that the imported milk powder and butter oil
were meant only for the metro dairies, significant amounts
of it ended up in the Kaira Cooperative's possession to be
used in high-valued foods and sold to unsuspecting customers.
And when the project had terminated, it was discovered that
despite the fact that Gujarat already had a highly developed
dairy economy, 20 percent of all Operation Flood funds had
been granted to it for its use.

The fact, however, that the country still required milk
powder imports indicated that indigenous production was nowhere near what was really needed or claimed. Thus, even
before the first OF project had ended in 1981, Kurien was
compelled to start Operation Flood II in 1978 for the principal reason that milk powder committed under OF I had already been used up and dairies needed more powder urgently.
(Resources were certainly more than adequate as the IDC had
more than 70 crores of rupees in various bank accounts.)

To cover up failed objectives more ambitious targets
were proposed. Operation Flood II would:

a) enable some 10 million farmers to build a viable self-maintaining dairy industry by mid-

1985;

b)   enabled farmers to raise a national milch
     herd of some 14 million crossbred cows
     and upgraded buffalos during the 1980s;

c)   erect a national milk grid, linking rural
     milksheds to major demand centers with
     urban populations, totaling 150 million;

d)   erect infrastructure, software, and hard-
     ware to support a national dairy industry;
     and

e)   with such improvements in production and
     marketing, enable milk and milk products
     to be a part of a stable, nutritionally
     adequate national diet with a per capita
     consumption of 180 grams per person during
     the 1980s.

While Operation Flood I had relied upon 42,000 tons of
butter oil and 126,000 tons of SMP (Skim Milk Powder), OF II
was based on further free supplies of 76,000 tons of butter
oil and 186,000 tons of SMP. Additionally, OF II was to
receive World Bank assistance to the tune of $150 million.
Later, it was decided to forego part of the World Bank credit
and ask the EEC for a further gift of 10,000 tons of SMP and
35,000 tons of butter oil. It will be recalled that in the
case of OF I, independence from SMP imports was promised
first in 1975, and then again in 1981. In the case of OF II,
according to the official documents the share of imported
supplies over the period of the project was to be as in the
following table:

TABLE 1

Share of Imported Supplies

1978-1979	1979-1980	1980-1981	1981-1982	1982-1983	1983-1984	1984-1985
9%	11%	15%	15%	8%	4%	2%

Source: *National Dairy Project, OF II*, Projects Appraisal Division, Planning Commission, Government of India, New Delhi, 1978.

What is the situation now in 1985? In 1984, the IDC/NDDB had contracted for SMP from a new source, the United States, in quantity of 20,000 tons. The project has now been officially extended to 1990! Except for Bombay, all of the other dairies are still hooked on imported powder. Bombay is *not*, truly speaking, an Operation Flood. OF I had merely funded two dairies in Maharashtra state, and OF II agreements with Maharashtra were only signed in 1984. Kurien was supposed to see that the four metro dairies achieved their full targets of indigenously produced milk by 1975. In 1984, he tried a new strategy to accomplish this at any cost. Fresh milk from smaller town dairies was transported over some distance to the four dairies, and the town dairies in turn were given imported SMP for their populations. In the process, 150 dairies became dependent on milk powder from abroad, and even then the metro dairies still remained dependent on imported milk powder. Thus, an autonomous dairy system has now been brought into a crippling dependence on the European dairy industry, and through a project that once guaranteed total independence!

On the production front, milk production may have risen

at a marginal level, but this increase is better credited to a naturally incremental livestock population rather than to better stock. How then was the shortfall in milk production made up? By draining milk from more and more remote rural areas; procurement and collection made up for production. In the cities, Kurien was able to provide urban consumers with the milk they wanted, without them knowing that the milk had been made available by depriving rural consumers. Operation Flood was thus based on "Operation Drain," in turn producing yet another converse result. Instead of improving milk consumption by all, it increased the consumption of some at the expense of many.

For most casual observers, it did seem as if milk production had increased since people in the cities saw more of it around. Capitalizing on this, the NDDB set out to claim credit for this "increased milk production." By 1982, it had hired an advertising agency to prepare graphs indi- cating that milk production had dramatically increased, the productivity of livestock had risen, and per capita consump- tion of milk had improved--all solely due to the project.

Official policy now justified this reduced accessibil- ity to rural areas through a nutritional theory that would do credit to apartheid regimes. Verghese Kurien has pub- licly stated, and also proposed in documents, that the rural poor actually do not need milk. They should sell all their milk to the rich and use the money to buy "cheaper" cereals and pulses. In its preamble to OF I, the WFP agreement spe- cifically states that "the development of animal husbandry will also provide the milk required for the population of whom 30 to 40 percent are vegetarians and whose only source of animal protein food is in the form of milk and milk

products."[8] The "Memorandum on Operation Flood II" specif-
ically states that as a result of the project, milk consumption per capita will increase to 180 grams and that *existing
disparities in consumption between urban and rural populations would be reduced.*[9] Thus, a project that began with·
the objective of improving the protein content of all diets
now officially claims that milk protein is not necessary for
a major portion of the population.

That the rich are benefiting in this "development"
project intended to help "poor farmers" is quite obvious.
The price of fresh milk in cities like Bombay has climbed
above Rs.6 per litre (whereas the price of a kilo of pulses
is now Rs.10). Kurien's pet baby, milk in expensive Tetra-
pak cartons, sells beyond even that price. Moreover, the
rich are now being offered milk in a bewildering variety of
forms--cheese, butter, ghee, shrikhand, milk powder, baby
foods, and chocolates. Thus, the rich, already well taken
care of as far as their protein requirements are concerned,
now have increased access to milk in many more forms, while
milk disappears from the diets of those who produce it. All
this is achieved in the name of development.

Why did this all happen? European citizens will be
dismayed to hear how their free stockpiles ended up for
other purposes than feeding those who were really in need.
But this is the tale of all development projects in the
Third World: the intermediate class, the middleman, the institutions, the society that stands between the real donors
and the ones in real need can always ensure that aid will
never reach the poor. Socioeconomic objectives are appended
to business propositions in order to entice the aid-giver.

All independent studies on Operation Flood had already indicated that dairying was not scale-neutral, as officials
claimed. If they ventured into the business, those who had
landed assets benefited more; those with less, made less;
and those with nothing, made nothing or lost.

Operation Flood: The Stark
Reality

What then, in sum, have been the major deleterious
effects of this grandiouse scheme?

As already stated, the traditional dairy system was
finding it hard to cope with the natural increase in the
number of animals. Efforts were being made to gradually reverse the balance. Of course, until some drastic action is
taken on the prime issue of a proper redistribution of assets and resources, even these efforts would not produce any
dramatic turnaround. Societies, however, do sense in some
instinctive way when they are moving perilously close to
self-extermination, and cautiously attempt to change, even
while their social structures--or distribution of economic
power--remain based on gross concepts of injustice.

Into such a system, OF has constituted a major Western-
inspired technological intervention. In order to enable the
Western system to grow, the traditional system is being undermined. Yet, from all evidence, the Western system itself
does not seem capable of fulfilling the country's needs.

The system is totally inappropriate--from the choice of
breeds to the question of concentrates for animals, which
are based on grains also consumable by people. (Even here,
only 35 percent of the compound feeds produced in the
country are consumed by cattle since farmers either cannot

afford them or do not rely on them; the rest is exported!)
In like manner, we are still propagating exotic breeds of
animals from Holland or America, even while Australia, Brazil, Bangladesh, and New Zealand are importing indigenous
Indian breeds.

What has been the result of all this development? As
we stated earlier, large masses of rural folk are being deprived of milk protein. Their jobs, involved in the processing of milk to produce ghee, have been transferred to
urban-based, capital-intensive plants, constructed to profit
European dairy transnationals. The European citizen has
been cheated of the satisfaction of seeing the results of
his or her generosity delivered to those in genuine nutritional need. The long-term coping ability of India's traditional dairy system, based on agricultural wastes and natural herbiage, has been severely compromised in favor of a
fodder-based system that will cut into the human population's requirements.

The rich farmers have become richer, and the wealthier
segments of the Indian population have access to all the
kinds of dairy products they once thought were only the purview of the Europeans. These segments now consider themselves truly civilized and "developed." As a result of the
increasing economic disparities in the villages conflicts
and tensions will increase, while on the milk-consumption
side tea will be drunk without milk, and *lassi* (a popular
cooling drink) dismissed as a relic of the past.

Even in the case of the rich farmer, it is not yet
clear whether he benefits from a project of this sort, which
encourages reliance on expensive, urban-produced inputs like
concentrates and veterinary medicines--still the preserve of

drug transnationals. Al.hough gross earnings seem to have risen, retained earnings are marginal, and this severe imbalance has led to the rise of major farmer agitations in several states in the country. Evidently, even if the rich farmers make money, they are not convinced that they are making *profits*. The dilemma governments face, however, is that any further increases in the milk price will reduce the market further in the cities.

Finally, even the urban consumer may be suffering because of the project: the milk that the Delhi dairy gets from Anand, Gujarat, is pasteurized thrice, and authorities have been caught adding hydrogen peroxide to the milk supplies in order to prevent them from spoiling over the vast distances they are transported. So the very notion of fresh whole milk has now been buried. And the ubiquitous presence of imported SMP has led to its being used in practically every dairy in the country--still another reason why fresh milk is a thing of the past.

No one knows all this better than Verghese Kurien and the officials of the NDDB/IDC. In the Third World, however, where democracies exert themselves merely once in five years, a few individuals vested with unimaginable powers can continue their policies without interruption from any source and irrespective of criticism. Operation Flood is, in fact, not merely a revolution in pure statistics (and the way in which these can be manipulated and sold to a gullible public). It is also an intensively media-created success. A film, *Manthan*, was made a few years ago on Verghese Kurien and Amul, and a sequel-- *Manthan II*--is now in the offing. Fantasy is required to eclipse, even if temporarily, the reasons why another revolution has failed.

Notes

1. Operation Flood (OF) consists of two projects. OF I began in July 1970, was to end in 1975, but was extended to 1981. OF II commenced in 1978, was to end in 1985, but was extended first to 1987 and now to 1990. The estimated budget for OF I is Rs.1160 million, and for OF II Rs. 4850 million. At current exchange rates, $1 is worth approximately Rs.12.

2. The National Dairy Development Board (NDDB) was registered in 1965 (under the India Societies Act of 1860) as a private society, outside the control of government. It functions as a dairy consultancy outfit, and has recently ventured into other agriculture-related activities, such as oilseeds, fruits, and vegetables. The Supreme Court this year agreed with a judgment of the Bombay High Court in December 1983, holding that the NDDB falls within the definition of "state." The Indian Dairy Corportion (IDC), incorporated in 1970, is a public sector corporation, formed to carry out Operation Flood. The board of directors of the NDDB and the IDC are identical. The chairman of both is Verghese Kurien.

3. Anand-pattern cooperatives are basically village-level, rural milk producer cooperatives, originally organized in the Anand Area of Gujarat. These village cooperatives next form a district-level union. A third and final tier becomes operative when unions join under a federation. This pattern of organizing milk marketing and production is now known as the "Anand model," supposedly to become the basis of replication under Operation Flood all over the country.

4. *Ghee*, a form of clarified butter, is extensively used in Indian cooking. *Shrikhand* is a popular Indian sweet made from milk.

5. Verghese Kurien in *Debonair*, March 1984. (Cited also in "Compendium of Recent Press Reports on Operation Flood--Vol. 11," Anand: National Dairy Development Board [NDDB], March 1984, pp. 86-87.)

6. "Terminal Evaluation Report on Project India 618--Milk Marketing and Dairy Development (Operation Flood I)," Rome: FAO/WFP, September 1981.

7. "Plan of Operations Agreed Upon Between the Government
    of India and the United Nations/FAO World Food Programme
    Concerning Assistance to a Project for Milk Marketing
    and Dairy Development" (WFP Project No. 618), Rome: FAO/
    WFP, March 1970. (Excerpted in Claude Alvares, ed.,
    Another Revolution Fails, Delhi: Ajanta Books Interna-
    tional, 1985, p. 252.)

8. Ibid., p. 1. (Alvares, ed., *op. cit.*, p. 251.)

9. "Memorandum on Operation Flood II," Anand: National
    Dairy Development Board (NDDB), 1977. (Alvares, ed.,
    op. cit., p. 264.)

References

Michael Halse, *Operation Flood: A Study*, Anand: National Dairy Development Board (NDDB), 1976.

Indian Dairy Corporation, *Annual Reports*, Baroda: IDC,
1971 onwards.

National Dairy Development Board, *Annual Reports*, Anand:
NDDB, 1966 onwards.

Operation Flood: Development or Dependence? Bombay:
Cite Publications, 1982. The first autonomous critical
study of Operation Floor I.

Another recent critical book on Operation Flood, which
radically questions the replicability of the Anand model and
the appropriateness of the OF project for India, is *Operation Flood: An Analysis of Current Indian Dairy Policy* by
Shanti George, Delhi: Oxford University Press, 1985. An
earlier paper by the same author, "Cooperatives and Indian
Dairy Policy: More Anand than Pattern," prepared for an
August 1983 workshop on Cooperatives and Rural Development
in Quebec, announces some of the central themes of the book
(Centre of Advanced Study in Sociology, Department of Sociology, University of Delhi).

Professor B.S. Baviskar, Head of the Department of
Sociology, University of Delhi, is also writing a book on

Anand cooperatives. A preliminary paper by Baviskar
(written with D.W. Attwood, "Rural Cooperatives in India,"
has been published in *Contributions to Indian Society*, Vol.
18, No. 1, 1984, pp. 85-107.

ECOLOGY VS. DEVELOPMENT: THE
STRUGGLE FOR SURVIVAL IN INDIA

Smitu Kothari

> They have taken our burial grounds, the bones of
> our ancestors, they have broken and submerged our
> sacred places, they have dug up our Mother. What
> else do we have left but to drown ourselves in
> drink?
>
> > As told to the author by Manko, a
> > Gond *Adivasi* (tribal), near the
> > site of the Malanjkand Copper
> > Mines, Madhya Pradesh.

Why are we silent? All around us thousands of people
are dying or being killed in what is largely man-made violence. Dramatic events like the Bhopal gas tragedy momen-
tarily open the conviently closed shutters of our consciousness. Yet, our collective responses have been sluggish,
disorganized, fragmented.

The silence continues, compounding the tragedy of the
poor, the marginalized and the weak in our country. Palla-
tives abound--official or independent. But in the final
analysis, it is the agony of the silence that prevails. The
tragedy continues.

This note outlines some of the crucial factors which
have created the crisis of survival for millions of people.
This is followed by an outline of the citizen's response by
way of individual and collective protest and struggle. A

concluding section sketches the challenges before us.

Resources for Survival

The struggle for survival relates essentially to the
control of resources--both natural and financial. Control
over the latter has usually permitted easier access to the
former. A significant part of our contemporary social history is therefore a document on the existing structures
which have legitimized and strengthened the exploitation
and utilization of natural resources.

This, in turn, has necessitated the establishment of
complex and diverse institutions, culminating in the modern
state.

The creation of these institutions at the top and
their control by a small elite have made it almost impossible for a broader process of participation to work. At
the same time, traditional structures of authority and
power have imposed serious limits on both the sustained
percolation of benefits to the poor and on the effective
assertion and articulation of their rights.

Those controlling the dominant institutions have been
able to harness resources and energy-intensive technologies.
These technologies have led to a minority of people achieving significant economic growth while undermining the material basis for the survival of the majority. Nevertheless,
the argument made soon after independence that poverty was
a consequence of "backwardness" and low production in the
agricultural and industrial sectors continues to be reas-
serted by the present regime--a regime which also claims
that only modern technological inputs in these sectors will

create higher "efficiency" and productivity, leading to higher rates of growth and to the removal of poverty.

Poverty itself is seen as technological problem for the nation as a whole, not the result of socio-economic and cultural conditions at the bottom. The consequence is paradoxically the reinforcement of the rich-poor divide. With increasing state subsidies which facilitate resource planning for the rich, the technocratic option directly implies that the poor must fend for themselves. Simultaneously, the poor are burdened with false dichotomies, such as the argument that you can either have food or forests, not both. Nature is not seen as a relatively infinite producer and provider but as something that has to be moulded and most often desecrated for short-term gains. Earlier, there was adequate scope for extracting surplus without necessarily undermining the productivity base. Second, the existing idea of scientific and technological growth has legitimized the dominant theories of growth and surplus generation. They have arrogantly endorsed the underlying assumption that solutions to problems are the prerogative of experts schooled in modern developmental thinking.

We would like to argue the other way--that the existing patterns of production and of energy and resource use have *created* the "threat to survival·" The introduction and spread of more "effective" technologies in areas like agriculture, forestry, and fishing has seriously undermined the physical and psychological survival of poor and marginal communities all over the world. And alongside this *biological* survival of marginal communities is the continuous threat to the survival of their cultures. The undermining of cultural plurality is thus built into the dominant model of "progress."

The threats are interwined: while cultures are sought to be brought under the homogenizing juggernaut, so are genetic resources; indeed, the two go together. The physical environment has never before faced as much man-created degradation as it does today. With the erosion of cultural diversity, what is also falling by the wayside is biological diversity. While environmental degradation has seriously threatened the survival of those dependent on it, the imposition of external technologies on this has disrupted the natural genetic diversities that took thousands of years to evolve.

The overall consequence of all this is a degradation that is almost irreversible. The resource base of more and more people is shrinking. Survival for many has become a daily struggle. What is worse, any demand to stop such "development" gets translated by the system into an act of confrontation and is dealt with through repression and genocide.

A systematic, sustained propagation of this model of development has created both a supportive middle class (whose needs and "greeds" continue to be progressively fulfilled) as also a growing enslavement of the consciousness of large numbers of people (including, unfortunately, that of a large section of the "masses"). Mass communication systems are used to establish ideological hegemony. Dominant interpretations of reality thus become *the only* interpretations of it, and anything that threatens the model threatens the consciousness of the relatively more articulate sections of society. In the final analysis, the aim of development appears to be to create a "universal middle class" condi-

tioned to accept the logic of the dominant institutions.
It is for these reasons that any major critique of the
model is sought to be contained, disregarded, and, if this
fails, crushed. Not only is legitimization of serious dissent prevented at all costs by the dominant classes, the
latter's own views are projected as that of the majority.
Thus, a dominant minority has acquired the character of a
majority in an unprecedented coup.

Destabilization and Official Apathy:
The Case of the Narmada Oustees

The Narmada River Valley project is a colossal construction scheme of 30 major dams, 135 medium dams, and
3,000 minor irrigation sites. The current estimates for the
entire project range from Rs.40 to 90 billion. But going by
cost revisions of one of the first dams under construction (Sardar Sarovar in Gujarat), the final cost is likely
to be over a staggering Rs.250 billion. Extensive project
plans have been drawn up and the project reports of the
first two dams to be built (Sardar Sarovar and Narmada Sagar,
the latter in Madhya Pradesh) glow about the benefits and
also attempt to provide detailed economic justifications for
the projects. Nevertheless, two glaring shortcoming of the
reports are the almost complete lack of assessment at the
planning stage itself of the environmental and the human
costs of the projects. This amounts to an almost conscious
evasion on the part of the government, as it has under-
valued the loss due to submergence of 375,000 hectares of
forests (including some of India's best deciduous forests),
of about 80,000 hectares of fertile agricultural land, and
of substantial grazing lands with their direct impact on

cattle and grazing populations. Also not computed is the irreversible loss of rare wild flora and fauna, the environmental impact of rigid industrialization and urbanization once the projects are underway and completed, the impact on changes in the cycle on human health, the cultural loss due to displacement, and so forth. Studies by independent groups (vis. Development or Destruction? by the Kalpavriksh group of Delhi) suggest that if these were tabulated, each of the dams on the river could turn out to be uneconomical.

With over one million people facing displacement due to the Narmada project, there has been pathetically little done to ensure full rehabilitation. While no comprehensive policy for the entire project exists, even individual dam-specific rehabilitation has so far been tardy. In Gujarat, were it not for action groups which have vigorously campaigned for full rehabilitation, the official attitude would have been clearer--that people in the way of developmental projects are expendable and that they must fend for themselves.

Let me briefly describe the rehabilitation of the oustees of the Sardar Sarovar project. A total of 219 villages will be eventually displaced (19 from Gujarat, 173 from Madhya Pradesh, and 27 from Maharashtra). The villagers from six of them in Gujarat that were the first disrupted were typically shown land 150 kilometers away--land that was rocky and almost non-cultivable. The oustees refused. The government then agreed to pay cash compensation (like elsewhere in the country, cash compensation was tabulated, at best, as current land prices for inferior quality land). Landlords knowing that hundreds were going to be forced to buy land in the area, substantially raised land prices thus making it impossible for the oustees to buy land. The result: a wide scattering of a relatively homo-geneous community.

For the above six villages, the government then attempted to lure the oustees by offering a consent award at the rate of Rs.11,000 per hectare. As the first in-stallment, Rs.6,250 was released, but most villagers were unable to buy land with this amount. Many entered into sale deeds in the hope that they would eventually get the second installment. Meanwhile, two years passed, the Additional Collector who had cleared the award was suddenly trans-ferred, and the second installment remained unpaid.

The collective experience of official apathy created a sense of anger and contributed to the empowerment of the villagers of the remaining 13 villages. Over the last two years, they have drawn up, along with local action groups, a comprehansive rehabilitation scheme and demanded its imple-mentation. The process of building a powerful chain of pressures grounded in Gujarat, but linking up with both the national and international groups, is a remarkable story of its own. (This will be examined later.)

What the process of "official" rehabilitation clearly illustrates (and this is reinforced by numerous case studies over the last 40 years from all over the country) are the following four points.

   a)   there is usually no comprehensive plans for
        rehabilitation when populations are dis-
        placed by development projects;

   b)   there is an almost total insensitity to-
        ward the prevailing social and cultural

processes of the people leading inexorably
to cultural annihilation;

c) wherever the displacement and disruption
are *visible* or the affected people *collec-
tively vocal*, adequate cash compensation
is given. Landless labor or those cultivating land over which no legal title ex-
ists--village commons, degraded forest
lands, semi-cultivable lands, etc.--end up
without even the cash compensation; and

d) land for land--especially cultivable land
with adequate irrigation--is almost never
provided and this forces the displaced
community to scatter in different directions.

It can be argued that greater care in rehabilitation
can avoid most of these problems. There is also the fact
that the benefits of projects such as Sardar Sarovar are
grossly exaggerated. If land is provided for land to all
oustees in well-irrigated or well-forested areas, and if the
entire group of displaced villages are settled as villages
(thereby not disrupting cultural continuities and social
relationships); if the costs of forests and land lost due to
submergence and other construction and infrastructural activity is computed; if the regular cost escalations are taken
into account; and, if the loss of agricultural production is
deducted from the *actual* benefits--the above contention would
be reinforced. And as has already been outlined, what of the
majority of oustees? They face the grim cycle of displacement, cultural destabilization, and impoverishment. And notwithstanding these massive consequences, they are never con-
sulted. In a project that so intimately affects them they
are expected at best to survive for a while.

Questioning Displacement: Dams
on the Koel-Karo Rivers

The Rs.6 billion, Koel-Karo (KK) hydroelectric project,
comprising of two dams on the Koel and Karo rivers of Bihar,
is another of the instances reflecting the crisis of survival.

Conceived in the early 1950s, the project was approved
by the Planning Commission in 1973 after preliminary sur-
veys. A report of the National Hydroelectric Power Corporation (NHPC), which is to construct the project, states that
since the Eastern region has been dependent on coal-based
thermal power, and since there are "operational difficulties
not only for optimum utilization but also by way of reli-
ability and quality of power supply," the KK project will
provide the needed power (71 mW) to stabilize the output.

The area facing disruption is primarily an Adivasi
area. Within months of the approval of the project, struggle committees were formed in some of the villages facing
submergence. In 1974, activists of the Jharkhard Mukti
Morcha and the Communist Party of India brought these village organizations under the common banner of the Koel-Karo
Jana Sangathana (the People's Organisation of Koel-Karo).

The official attitude was revealed in the Detailed
Project Report (DPR) of 1973, which only cursorily mentioned
compensation and rehabilitation. They were mere financial
gestures with no mention of resettlement or of providing land
and other supportive facilities to the displaced. Ironically, a provision was made for providing land for huts. The
implication was that with the cash compensation and a postage
stamp plot of land, a hut would be constructed and the dispossessed would then have to fend for themselves. The Sanga-

thana now states that 15,000 families in about 100 villages
will be adversely affected. The government, on the other
hand, claims that these figures are exaggerated and land of
only 7,573 families in 50 villages will have to be acquired
(approximately 20,000 hectares). It is interesting to note
that to date no comprehensive survey of the affected area
has been conducted.

In 1975, the Sangathana appealed to the government to
outline its rehabilitation program. There was no concrete
response. Instead, three years were allowed to pass, and in
1978 the government decided to go ahead by opening an approach road to the dam site. The Adivasis barricaded the
road, effectively blocking access to the site. This forced
the Deputy Commissioner of Ranchi to draw up a rehabilitation scheme. The process of thrashing out this scheme took
two years. The Sangathana responded by offering its criticisms.

Once again, there was no response. Suddenly, a year
later in October 1981, a fresh official proposal was sent to
the Adivasi representatives, outlining a compensation scheme
(with no mention of rehabilitation) and a plan to absorb one
member of each family in a government job. By this time,
however, the Sangathana had also realized the official intention and demanded land for land, legal protection of traditional Adivasi rights and customs, and a scheme for comprehensive rehabilitation.

The government did not acceed to these demands. In
1983, however, in what was projected to be a major gesture,
it upgraded its own token cash compensation to between Rs.
3,200 and Rs.8,000 per acre. The real intention was, however, obvious from the fact that after ten years of listening

to the basic demands of the Adivasis, all that was added to
the enhanced cash compensation was that there would be a
reservation in Class III and Class IV jobs in Chhota Nagpur
area, including within the NHPC. On the question of land
for land, an offer was made to rehabilitate the displaced in
neighboring villages and to meet welfare needs in the rehabilitation areas. Throughout this period, the government
tried to influence opinion in the area both by parroting the
gains of the project and by attempting to influence and divide the community. Although it has, to an extent, succeeded in this effort, significant proportions of the population question the very need for the project, arguing that
if the intention is to benefit the local people, a fraction
of the total outlay could be differently used to significantly alter the amount of land under irrigation by smaller
check dams, afforestation, etc. The voice of such opposition remains unheard. Tension continues within the Sangathana between those who accept the inevitability of the dams
and want comprehensive rehailitation and those who do not
want the dams.

For ten long years, the people around Koel-Karo have
been kept in a limbo, suspended as it were between imminent
impoverishment and their present life of subsistence. And
then, suddenly last summer, in order to weaken the resolve
of the Adivasis, armed constabulary was sent in and rumors
spread that if the people did not accept cash compensation,
they would be thrown out "with neither compensation nor
jobs."

Researchers and social workers in the area concede the
fact that the entire process has created tremendous inse-
curity in the Adivasis besides forcing them to break up into

factions, each supporting different levels of the negotiations. If the government uses force to go ahead in this
climate, there is general fear that total chaos will prevail
and, once again, the Adivasis will pay the price for wanting
to retain their collective identify and dignity.

Rather than conceding to the demand of reappraising the
entire scheme, a news item in *New Republic*, June 23, 1984,
has confirmed that a resolution was passed in January 1984
in which the Chief Minister gave the green signal to the
project even if it required the use of force or resorting to
firing. Two Adivasis then filed a petition in the Supreme
Court. It is relevant here to quote from the petition:

> The attempt of the (government) to resort to
> violence...smacks of the fact that they (gov-
> ernment) consider the tribal communities as
> secondary citizens and in the way of so-
> called development. (The government) feels
> that the tribals are *not a part* of develop-
> ment of this nation but a hinderance. The
> tribals of the area have a deep-rooted cul-
> ture and economic life associated with land
> and to tear them off from their land is to
> separate the blood from their body.

The official insensitivity was apparent when the Commissioner who was negotiating with the Adivasis, offered to buy
off the religious place of the tribals. The Adivasis said
that had such an offer been made by an outsider to any other
religious community, there would have been riots. They con-
clude by arguing that, "rehabilitation as a mode of charity
cannot be accepted anymore" and that "the system of cash compensation instead of land for land in the case of tribals,
needs to be declared illegal and unconstitutional since that
only brings in slow death to the economic and cultural life
of the tribals."

The militancy of the activists of the Jana Sangathana (even though there are two groups within it--one accepting that the dams should be built and, therefore, comprehensive and full rehabilitation should be implemented *before* the project starts and the other questioning the logic of the project itself), has its roots in the missionary activity in the area since the mid-1800s. What is of crucial significance is that they are raising their collective voice against the state treating them as second-class citizens whose lives can be disrupted for the so-called larger good. As the above petition argues: "It is unfortunate that (the government) instead of understanding the tribal reality, is resorting to force to drive them away as stray animals giving trouble to (official) projects."

If most of the displaced and disrupted communities do not benefit, and if the other related costs (ecological, etc.) are so enormous, who does benefit?

While the obvious beneficiaries are the traders, contractors, and richer tribals, it has been argued that the increased area that would be brought under perennial cultivation and power generation would provide a boost in food and industrial output, besides raising the standard of living in the areas where the projects came up.

Does increased food output necessarily guarantee greater access to food and power to the bottom 50 percent of our society? A brief look at the food and hunger situation can easily explode this assumption.

Food and Hunger Situation

Over the past five years, the government has been claiming that it has achieved self-sufficiency in food. The food grain production in 1983-1984 was stated to be 152 million tons--approximately 220 kilograms per year for every person in the country.

This statistic, however, hides the continuing struggle for survival, affecting millions of people who not only do not have the money to purchase food but who also suffer from chronic undernourishment. The claim of self-reliance also conceals the fact that the increased food grain production is dependent on an agricultural strategy of high-yielding varieties, fertilizers, and pesticides--along with the reliance on transnational corporations, Western experts, and sizeable imports of technology.

Estimates of *rural* poverty in India indicate that the percentage of the population below the poverty line has stood close to 60 during the last 20 years. Although recent studies claim a reduction as a consequence of the massive outlays in rural development programs, these studies do not state whether those who benefited have acquired permanently improved economic status. Other indicators suggest that modern food strategies have done little to alleviate the debilitating aspects of poverty--over 40 percent of the population still consumes less than 2,250 calories per day; over 85 percent of children under five are below the normal state of nutrition; 30,000 children turn blind every year due to Vitamin A deficiency; the number of malnourished people in the country expands annually by about 6 million people.

The other factor which perpetuates this state of affairs is the inequality in the distribution of resources. Of the 80 million rural households, 27.5 percent do not own any land; 32.5 percent operate small holdings (below 2.5 acres); 30 percent operate medium holdings (2.5 to 9.99 acres); while 10 percent operate holdings of 10 acres and above. *Stated differently, 60 percent of the bottom rural households operate only 9 percent of the land, while the top 10 percent operate 53 percent of land.*

The struggle for survival of the bottom 60 percent gets sharpened by the discriminatory benefits enjoyed by the top 10 percent who not only corner a larger share of irrigation waters but also receive the benefits of subsidized fertilizers, bank loans, etc. At the bottom, there is thus a vast strata of landless or near landless laborers who own and control almost no productive assets. *They toil to produce food but their low material base keeps them from meeting their own nutritional requirements.* The distress of agricultural laborers becomes aggravated when, due to unfavorable weather or a natural calamity, a bad harvest results.

Simultaneously, with more and more land being brought under Green Revolution technology, there are two other consequences. Greater mechanization leads to declining labor use. More importantly, the crop mix changes leading to a decline in the production of coarse cereals and pulses. The lot of vast masses of the rural poor laborer then gets worse.

Further, the intensive use of chemical fertilizers erodes soil nutrients, posing an additional threat to both future food production and the marginal peasant households dependent on land for survival. The magnitude of the problem can be gauged from the fact that over 23 million tons of soil nutrients are lost every year--75 percent due to chemical input-based agriculture.

Briefly, therefore, the modern agricultural strategy has increased rural contradictions, the pauperization of the marginal peasantry and forced the migration of large numbers of landless laborers. As with the current defense of "industrialization," the argument that in the future, increased productivity and income will absorb the marginal populations has been proven essentially false--not only due to the reasons mentioned above but also to the fact that nowhere in the country do large numbers of people control resources. In addition, the quality and range of access to these resources has declined, either due to environmental destabilization or to the new agricultural strategies.

In growing areas of the country, one response to this continuing degradation in the quality of life and the exploitation by landed interests and other exploiter groups is a wide variety of assertions. They range from small localized actions for realizing minimum wages or for strengthening organic agriculture to broadbased movements against monocultural plantations. There are, of course, other major movements--those that are fighting for greater control over both access to agricultural inputs and for better procurement prices. While the latter do not question the modern agricultural methods, the former do, as also the continuing authority of centralized bureaucracies which control resources and decide the direction of agricultural development.

Silence and Struggle

I have briefly described random instances to show the

exploding crisis of survival faced by people, cultures, and the environment. Each of the above examples can be further strengthened through descriptions of similar trends in other areas. And yet, most of us remain silent.

Except some. Scattered all over the country, groups and individuals are waging a resistance--brave efforts in the face of the relentless juggeranaut of development. The actors are politically weak and relatively disorganized groups of poor and marginal communities, whose resource needs are lowest and who live supported mainly by products of nature--often outside the market system--communities whose survival depends on the conservation and judicious use of nature's resources.

The arenas of resistance are numerous--from the now extensively publicized Chipko movement and its counterpart, the Appiko movement in Karnataka, to resistance to the Silent Valley project in Kerala; from the opposition to the Tehri (Uttar Pradesh), Koel-Karo (Bihar), and Inchampalli-Bhopalpatnam (Madhya Pradesh, Andhra Pradesh, and Maharashtra) dams to the movements for full rehabilitation, where entire communities are displaced as in the Sardar Sarovar project on the Narmada River; from the protests against limestone mining in the Doon Valley (*Lokayan Bulletin* 3:2) to the peasant movements to "Save the Soil" in Karnataka (Save the Soil Campaign--*Lokayan Bulletin* 3:3), and in the Tawa and the Ghatprabha-Malaprabha area where people are organizing to resist the growing waterlogging caused by irrigation projects meant for water-intensive cash crops; from the movements against the pollution of rivers like the Chambal (Madhya Pradesh), the Tungabhadra (Karnataka), the Chaliyar (Kerala) to the struggles against air pollution caused by industries

and construction-related activity like mechanized stone
crushing; from communities fighting the alienation of their
land all over the country to those asserting the need for
the implementation of existing legislation (and the Constitution) as in the peasant movements in Bihar or the struggles against the non-implementation of the Employment Guarantee Scheme in Maharashtra; from the movements to fight for
the rights of traditional fisherfolk as in Kerala (ocean-
going) and Dhanbad (river-based) to the fairly widespread
opposition to the new textile policy which threatens the
livelihood of thousands of handloom weavers and producers of
cotton.

While these movements, protests, and resistances continue, wherever they have proved effective *thus necessitat-
ing change*, there has been a counter-resistance. This
"backlash" has taken many forms--vilification, inspired mass
hysteria against individuals and groups, attempts to divide
resistance by offering concessions, and, when all else fails,
outright lawless repression (direct or indirect). The nature of the backlash is directly linked to the national visi-
bility of the specific struggle. The less visible, the
easier it is to crush.

There are, in this context, crucial lessons to be
learned from the protest movement around the Sardar Sarovar
dam on the Narmada River. After the politicization that
took place among the affected people because of the non-
payment of the second compensation installment and the rude
and apathetic behavior of the officials, several local
action groups took it upon themselves to struggle along with
the Adivasis for a *just* settlement in the place of the displacement that the dam would cause.

Initially, through village meetings and press statements, the issues were raised and debated. Corrective actions were sought from the officials and in many cases, when this was not forthcoming or was delayed, resistance grew and consolidated. For instance, the official attitude made it necessary to file a petition in the High Court of Gujarat on the issue of the provision of compensation.

With this rise in local consciousness, which the planners saw only as impediments to the project, came the realization that localized struggle had to be linked both laterally within the area and vertically with sensitive bureaucrats, support organizations, and the press--both in the state capital of Ahmedabad and in Delhi.

Ironically, the other "external" factor that helped was the involvement of the World Bank as the primary source of loans for the project. Over the past decade, the Bank had been coming under fire from its member governments regarding the human and environmental costs of the projects that it funds. It was this adverse publicity, coupled with a militant and articulate action group in the field (linked with major support organizations like Kalpavriksh and Lokayan), that forced the Bank to appoint an independent consultant. Simultaneously, the activists and support groups wrote to several organizations in the U.K. and the U.S. who, in turn, raised the issue with the Bank.

After a series of meetings at all levels, the consultant recommended a serious effort at primary data collection to be followed by a comprehensive scheme of rehabilitation which included, among other things, the provision of land for land and for the minimization of the psycho-cultural and economic disruption inherent in displacement.

However, in spite of assurances given to the potential oustees and the World Bank, the Gujarat government continued to reduce its responsibilities toward rehabilitation. This attitude was highlighted early this year, when it gave permission to one of the dam contractors to remove the top soil from the land belonging to villagers of one village for construction of dikes. Prior to this, it had hurriedly obtained thumbprints and signatures of some of the villagers by promising them cash compensation. Realizing the long-term loss of livelihood, a petition was filed in the High Court on behalf of the villagers by the Vahini (a non-governmental organization providing support to tribals). A stay order was granted but subsequently, with the change of the Chief Justice (who was hearing the case), the case was thrown out. The petitioners went up in the appeal to the Supreme Court where, at present, the case is pending.

The Vahini activists assert that the Gujarat government continues to behave in this way primarily because the "concessions" that they grant to the oustees of the Sarder Sarovar dam will become precedents, both for the nearly million people facing eventual displacement and for other similar projects which cause disruption.

Following the same logic, but in the opposite direction, the activists feel that what has been of crucial importance in their relatively successful struggle is the establishment of links at all levels, from the local to the international. While the Gujarat government has tried to discredit or circumvent the peoples' initiatives for better rehabilitation, the presence of a strong movement has prevented this from happening.

The results at Sardar Sarovar are by no means spectac-

ular. But valuable lessons have been learned, new precedents have been set, and new directions have been provided
to the continuing struggle for survival--directions which
need to be widely diffused and shared.

Struggles like that of the Adivasi oustees of Sardar
Sarovar, as also most of those mentioned above, raise questions critical to the struggle for survival. It is important to understand them in the vitiated atmosphere of irre-
sponsive and decadent politics and the near-complete apathy
among the media and the intellectuals to the continuing erosion of sources of resistance. These initiatives, therefore,
represent a powerful current for a different way of ordering
society.

Fundamentally, these efforts question a system which
perpetuates over-consumption of a few instead of satisfying
the basic needs of many, and in which there is a transfer of
production from, for instance, of artisans to resource and
energy-intensive industries incapable of absorbing those
that they displace. This is a system committed to current
models of development that destroy resources and divert them
from the needs of the poor, and also creates the conditions
for impoverishment and conflict. It is a system where growth
is contingent on deprivation, where integration into the
larger economy implies destruction of local resources and
displacement of local populations, and where the abstract
goal of "industrialization" concretely means unemployment of
millions. In this kind of system, moving into the future com-
pels dumping millions into the dustbin of history.

What is being therefore attempted in the scores of
initiatives is to both arrest these processes of resource
destruction and of "development causing underdevelopment,"

and to work *toward a new politics* which could reverse these trends. This reversal, currently demonstrated by many groups all over the country, is geared toward respecting and establishing ecological and cultural plurality--toward lives, livelihoods, environments, and cultures, free from the threat of degradation and annihilation.

And so while the silence of most of us becomes more deafening, elsewhere in many corners of the country it is being pierced by new voices. Are we capable of participating in this process of orchestrating these diffuse and often mute voices toward a cresendo? If we are not, if we are unable to prevent the marginal and weak and our own resource base from going under, there need be no doubt that the silence will engulf us--all of us.

V. IMPLICATIONS FOR ACTION

Editors' Note

ACTION IMPLICATIONS OF "FAILED"
RURAL DEVELOPMENT PROJECTS

One of the major causes of rural poverty in the Third
World is rural development that ostensibly seeks to alleviate such poverty but, in fact, serves other purposes and
interests. A truly careful and systematic examination of
the distribution of costs and benefits--both within the
country concerned and outside, if external agencies and resources are involved--is likely to reveal, at best, little
or no impact on rural poverty and, at worst, further impoverishment of the rural population.

This kind of situation is all the more difficult to
deal with since it appears, on the face of it, that the
major actors in such development initiatives--whether they
be government officials or technocrats within the country,
or representatives of industrialized country donor agencies--
present themselves as having the best interest of the rural
poor at heart. The two preceding papers have provided case
studies of four such projects in India: Operation Flood, the
Narmada River Valley project, the Koel-Karo hydroelectric
project, and Indian government projects to obtain self-
sufficiency in food through utilization of high-input Green
Revolution technologies.

Given these circumstances, what can participatory

organizations of the rural poor, social actions groups, and persons sharing their concerns do? The first step is to undertake a detailed analysis of the actual distribution of costs and benefits over a long enough period of time to be able to demonstrate just who gains and who loses. The length of time is crucial because the initial picture presented by one of these development projects often makes it appear that the rural poor actually are benefiting, whereas, over time, those who have in the past oppressed and exploited the poor will once again begin to appropriate, through one means or another, the lion's share of the benefits. It is also important that this examination be both comprehensive and reach out beyond the country involved to look at what is beginning in the donor country or countries. Operation Flood illustrates this point well because the major beneficiaries of that project in the end have proved to have been European dairy producers and transnational dairy equipment manufacturers. Likewise, the exporters of the technology and inputs used in Green Revolution agriculture have profited from the continuing reliance of HYVs on chemical inputs.

The next step is ordinarily one of exposure of the true state of affairs. This task is all the more difficult as it involves challenging the seemingly honorable motives and behavior of the key actors in such rural development projects. The media at all levels--local, state or provincial, national, and international--obviously have a key role to play in such exposure.

Exposure is best accompanied by the advocacy of some concrete and positive alternatives. In the case of Operation Flood, many small and marginal farmers have been drawn

into dairy cooperatives that, over time, serve more and more
the interests of those involved in processing and marketing
the milk products in urban areas, and less and less the
needs and concerns of the primary producers. PORPs and SAGs
should address themselves to helping poor farmers delink
from such organizational structures and forming alternative
structures more responsive to their needs.

Where large numbers of poor persons have been displaced
through rural development projects from their traditional
means of support, PORPs and SAGs must work toward obtaining
alternative means of livelihood for these people and ensuring recognition of responsibility on the part of government
for facilitating (and, at the very least, not hindering)
such means.

Yet another action strategy involves both rural and
urban-based social action groups, depending upon where products generated through a rural development project are being
sold. Again, to use the illustration of Operation Flood,
one of its major purposes has been to "modernize" the manufacture and marketing of dairy products in large cities,
thus creating an opportunity for those concerned with serving the cause of economic justice to organize consumer boy-
cotts.

Still another action strategy involves efforts to
improve the quality and productivity of traditional methods
and systems, without abandoning these methods and systems
altogether to so-called modern alternatives which often deprive the rural poor of control over even very meager productive resources. Yet, traditional methods are frequently
not very productive, and it is this consideration that gives
much of the appeal to "scientific" interventions in poor

peoples' lives in the name of development. "Join our scheme, and we will double your yields," is the promise often made by bureaucrats advocating such interventions. Such an initiative often involves seeking the help of groups of scientists and technologists who are genuinely committed to working with the rural poor and who have technical knowledge and skills relevant to the task of improving traditional productive systems.

DEVELOPING LEGAL STRATEGIES TO HELP
COMBAT RURAL IMPOVERISHMENT: USING
HUMAN RIGHTS AND LEGAL RESOURCES

Clarence Dias and James Paul

Introduction

The reports in this volume are illustrative of a much
larger body of literature. They portray some of the impoverishing effects of "development" activities undertaken or
promoted by international actors (transnational corporations,
the World Bank, or other international agencies) in collaboration with national actors (governmental bodies and local
firms). They depict, for example, some of the harms caused
by activities designed to transnationalize the production and
marketing of cash crops: landlessness; indebtedness; exploitation of rural laborers; introduction of hazardous products
(e.g., pesticides) which inflict impoverishing injuries upon
rural families; the degradation of natural environments and
food systems on which rural people rely for survival. They
show how technologies now being developed (notably biotechnologies) threaten replication of these kinds of harms, perhaps on an even more massive scale.

While these results have been widely portrayed few com-
mentators have asked: what can the victims--and those who
identify and work with them--do to prevent and redress these
harms?

The question focuses attention on organized, collective

self-help strategies, including the development of law and
legal resources to enable victim groups to protect themselves. These efforts are surely important; for it is often
unrealistic to assume that governments--even benign ones--
will lead the way in developing law to protect victim groups.
Indeed, governmental bodies (e.g., "public corporations")
are frequently participants in the very activities which
cause many of the harms described above. Other agencies
often lend encouragement, overt or passive, to private enterprise projects which are seen (by government) to promote economic growth, revenues, and other desired kinds of "development," but which also often inflict impoverishing harms on
large numbers of rural people in the process. Moreover, governments often seem insensitive to the plight of those harmed
by "development" projects. These victim groups usually lack
access to the media, politics, and law; and hence they lack
power to articulate grievances and demand preventive measures
and compensation for injuries inflicted. If governments are
to be induced to act, it is first necessary to empower victims with rights to demand remedial measures. Organized
efforts at grassroots levels to assert these rights, helped
by support and social action groups, may be essential if responsive law is to be developed, if remedies are to be enforced.

Of course, it is difficult in many countries to help
victims mobilize, and to generate in more elite circles the
concern, collaboration, and resources (notably legal resources) needed to support their efforts. However, in recent
years, victims, support groups, and international non-governmental organizations have begun to work with grassroots groups
and demand protections. These organizations, aided by activist

scholars and professionals, can make human rights law an important feature of their struggles. There is growing recognition, prompted by tragedies such as the Bhopal disaster, that the victims of development harms *must* enjoy powers to protect themselves if they are to be protected at all.

The human rights approach emphasized here is directed to those concerns: to the need to empower victims to demand remedial measures in order to realize "universal" rights promised by numerous international conventions (as well as by national constitutions and other sources of law) and by the rhetoric of development plans and official ideologies. These efforts must, of course, be country specific. Knowledge and understanding of the harms and harm-causing conduct associated with different kinds of international development projects must be generated by lawyers and other specialists working *with* those they seek to help. Rights to be protected from conduct which causes harms must be asserted in a variety of forums, but these rights must be formulated by victim groups and used to empower *them* to resist the wrongs inflicted upon them. Our purpose, here, is to show how this approach can be pursued by suggesting some illustrative lines of action.

Three kinds of tasks are discussed:

1. Identifying some harms (such as landlessness) which are frequent outcomes of particular international development projects; and identifying practices of both international and local actors which frequently cause those harms.

2. Developing self-help strategies to prevent these wrongs.

3. Developing law, notably human rights law,
    and legal resources to promote those strat-
    egies.

Identifying Harms and Harmdoers

An "international development project" (as we use the
term) denotes an undertaking involving some form of collaboration between local and international actors. These projects
frequently impose social costs on the rural poor even when
they bring visible benefits to others. Some are so fraught
with serious, foreseeable risks to the rural poor that the
very decision to proceed with the project without first en-
listing the participation of those bound to be affected, and
then devising full protections for their interrests, becomes
a wrong in itself. Examples include: projects to convert
both land and people to the production of export cash crops;
projects to build big dams or irrigation systems, airports or
major highways; projects to introduce new agricultural technologies and methods of production which are labor displacing
and far more costly compared with traditional methods.

In this section, we first describe some of the impoverishing harms which regularly accompany these kinds of projects, and second, some practices (of those who design, manage, or support the projects) which contribute causally to
these harms.

(1) Landlessness:

Some development projects (e.g., dams and plantations)
require transfers of large amounts of land to corporate or
governmental bodies from smallholders who are seldom beneficiaries of the project proposed.

The papers of Smitu Kothari and Caesar Espiritu vividly

portray the practices which governments and powerful firms use to wrest land from smallholders. Their land is invariably taken by some form of coercion: sometimes under the purported authority of an official expropriation; often by recourse to misrepresentation, threats, or force. Poor, ill-educated people are vulnerable to these tactics. Lacking legal and political resources, they lack power to protect their rights to the land they occupy. Indeed, those rights are often difficult to define, prove, and enforce under the terms of official law. Often smallholders do not own, out-right, the land they cultivate. They may possess it as "tenants" of another; or they may hold it under a system of customary tenure peculiar to their village or region. Sometimes they are seen as "squatter" occupants of valuable, "vacant" lands "owned" by the state. Yet, whatever status is ascribed to them, the families in possession, may in fact have lived on the land for generations, and, in any event, they depend on their rights of possession for basic livelihood and for their way of life.

It is all too easy to discount the rights of illiterate occupants who lack written records to support their claims; it is even easier to ignore the particular rights which other family members, notably wives, may also enjoy (by custom) in lands nominally possessed by a male "household head." Even when project planners avow the intention to provide fair re-imbursement, those charged with implementation often lack the time, resources, and processes needed to sort out the interests which will be destroyed by the taking and calculate the costs to be compensated. In any event, when reparation is provided, it is usually inadequate.

As Smitu Kothari's study shows, the harms inflicted on

families made landless with little or no compensation can, indeed, be serious. The land taken is usually a basic source of family food as well as income; it is also a source of security, status, and dignity; it is the basis for a distinct human community, often very old. Families made landless are left rootless and dependent. Thus, it is difficult to calculate the consequences and liquidate the damages when people are pushed from their holdings. Incentives to do so will rarely be strong unless responsible actors are held accountable for the full range of costs they inflict.

National and international "development actors" contribute to the infliction of these harms in a variety of different ways.

Private firms (seeking to establish plantations or other schemes for large-scale production) use, or condone, various forms of coercion or deception to acquire lands they need. Sometimes small farmers are promised lucrative employment and persuaded to sell or lease for a sum which cannot begin to compensate the losses they will suffer. Frequently corporate agents, or others acting independently, use threats to force cheap sellouts or violence to force eviction. Through bribes or other corruption, local officials are often enlisted in these enterprises.

Governmental bodies contribute in a variety of ways to the lawless processes which make people landless and impoverished. Government corporations are frequently joint venturers in projects to establish plantations. They, or other bodies, award concessions to private firms; they condone unlawful methods of land acquisition. They make unilateral official declarations that the land needed for these projects is "vacant," "public" land, and the occupants "squatters" with no rights at all.

When expropriation is undertaken, governmental bodies charged with implementation often find themselves under heavy pressure to reduce costs and expedite timetables. Usually there is little effort to investigate and understand the position of occupants and their system of land tenure. Their objections to the project are rarely heard, usually suppressed. The lands in question, or large portions, may be declared unoccupied and evictions ordered. Where compensation is promised, the process all too often lacks rules essential to assure fair reparation for those evicted. The burden is cast upon occupants to prove the existence of their holdings, and the proof required is difficult, at best, to produce. The formulae for determining compensation are set unilaterally. The fund set aside to defray awards is often woefully inadequate to pay for all the costs inflicted. In essence the process is lawless: the absence of clear, published procedures to protect occupants enables government to run roughshod over them.

Sometimes governments promise to resettle the evacuees on other public lands, in lieu of compensation. Recorded experiences portray the many difficulties inherent in these schemes. "Public" lands earmarked for resettlement may in fact already be occupied by others; or they may be vacant because they cannot be used productively by anyone, at least unless other resources and infrastructure are provided. Other harms occur, for example, the loss of a crop or a growing season, and hence vital subsistence. These and other costs are usually imposed on victims without compensation. Again, it appears that very little law governs resettlement schemes.

International actors, such as the World Bank and
private firms, are often involved in large-scale development
projects as providers of technical services and finance; the
terms of this assistance are negotiated and set out in elaborate agreements which establish a very important part of
the "law" (such as it is) which governs the project. Thus,
when it negotiates agreements, the Bank is in a position to
require, before any other action is taken, appropriate procedures to assure protection of the interests of those affected adversely by the project. Obviously, full protection
of their interests should begin with steps to permit their
participation in all of the crucial decisions governing the
project--ranging from whether it should be undertaken at all,
and if so, then how, to a full and fair calculation of all of
its social costs and appropriate guarantees for compensating
those who otherwise must bear them. But in fact these agreements are treated as secret by the parties who negotiate
them--rather than a source of rights to the foreseeable
victims of the project.

(2) Indebtedness:

Many development projects are designed to encourage
smallholders to convert from traditional small-scale, multi-
crop farming with emphasis on self-provisioning to the production of a single, export cash crop. Credit is an essential element in this process. Smallholders cannot participate in "Green Revolutions," or similar kinds of agricultural
change, without loans to pay for the seeds, fertilizers, pesticides, and other inputs required. Accordingly, international "development actors" collaborate with local ones to
encourage borrowing in order to promote the planned agricultural transformation.

Smallholders are particularly vulnerable to the harms
which indebtedness may bring. Once made dependent on credit
they become vulnerable to those who supply it. When they
cannot bargain over terms--rates of interest, schedules for
repayment, security--they lose control of their farms and
labor. The danger is compounded when new risks are encoun-
tered: the risk that the new crop to be grown may prove unsuitable to the environment, that the weather or the market
may fail, that expert advice given through extensions may
prove fatally flawed. When these or similar misfortunes
occur, indebtedness all too often leads to impoverishment,
and sometimes virtual enslavement to creditors.

The harms inflicted by indebtedness are widespread
through many parts of the Third World--yet seldom portrayed
in reports which view events through the eyes of those who
suffer these harms. Usual discussions of agricultural
credit reflect the concerns of official agencies which seek
to provide it: smallholders are seen as "the problem,"
rather than as people forced by circumstances beyond their
control into dependency on suppliers of credit. Study and
portrayal of the various forms of indebtedness imposed on
smallholder cash crop producers--and viewed from *their* per-
spective--is an urgent need. Doubtless such studies would
show how, when borrowers fall in arrears, they become further
locked into cash crop production; how they lose control of
their land, and ultimately, in many cases, possession of it.

Many activities, conducted or condoned by both governments and international organizations, contribute to these
outcomes. International organizations encourage initiation
of credit programs managed by state or parastatal agencies.
The intention may be to provide credit on liberal terms. But

it later develops that the costs of the program and pathologies of administration make it too burdensome to continue.
The terms of government lending are suddenly hardened unilaterally. Or the "liberalized credit" program is abandoned,
and the intended beneficiaries, already made dependent on
annual provision of credit, are forced to find alternative
sources. Private moneylenders and "big" farmers may provide
loans needed--but at the cost of usurious interest rates and
surrender of the control of land as security. TNCs, or their
local surrogates, may offer "package," "adhesion" contracts:
inputs (often the TNCs' own products) are provided on credit
in exchange for the farmers' promise to produce for the company at prices fixed by it, with the loan deducted from the
farmers' "profits." Government commodity corporations engage
in similar practices, using extension agents, state-managed
cooperatives, and other devices to persuade or coerce farmers
into production schemes. Frequently these corporations are
mismanaged; payments to farmers for crops already produced
are delayed, aggravating the problems of indebtedness. The
risks of bad advice, crop failure, declining markets, rising
input costs are known in advance by those who promote production schemes--or at least they are foreseeable. Invariably,
these risks are thrust upon farmers who have no means to
insure against them.

(3) Exploitation:

As Caesar Espiritu's reports show, some development
projects depend on cheap labor. Landless people, members of
families yoked with debt or otherwise impoverished become
workers in agribusiness enterprises.

The forms of their employment vary widely. Some are
employed as casual wage workers. In other settings, where

demands for heavy labor fluctuate with the season, agribusinesses employ migrant laborers; they are often recruited and
supervised by intermediaries (e.g., "labor contractors").
In still other settings, the company may use "sharecropping,"
"putting out" schemes, or "production contracts" to convert
small farmers into producers of the crops they need. For
some kinds of work, women or children are traditionally em-
ployed--and, of course, paid at depressed wages.

Whatever the form of the "employment," the workers are
usually very vulnerable to exploitation. They are often illiterate and vulnerable to cheating. If the workers are
landless, they are usually totally dependent on employment
with the firm for income enabling survival, and this total
dependency means that they will accept without protest the
conditions on which work is offered; for if they do not,
others who are just as desperate for the work will eagerly
(if not happily) accept the terms. Similarly, small farmers,
already pressed by indebtedness and lacking bargaining power,
may "agree" to the terms of "production contracts" which are
offered, indeed dictated, by the company.

The kinds of abuses which occur are described by
Espiritu, and indeed in countless reports on labor for agribusiness in Third World settings. While these wrongs are notorious, they are widely neglected.

The forms of exploitation are as ingenious as the modes
of employment. It is easy, of course, to depress wages and
cheat illiterate and marginal workers. Migrants are given
advances or "credit" to cover the costs of their transport
and maintenance. "Interest" is then added to the "debt" and
factored into calculations of work owed and wages due. Re-
cruiters and supervisors practice other abuses--cloaking

their exactions in some legal form such as a "commission" or a "loan." Trade union activity on behalf of workers is suppressed--sometimes by coercion, sometimes by corrupting the hierarchies of national unions which purport to represent agrarian workers but have no real incentives to do so. Work conditions in some of these enterprises are notoriously unhealthy or otherwise dangerous. Hazardous machinery and other products such as pesticides are increasingly used; they may be inherently dangerous, or at least dangerous when misused--a probable event when warnings are inadequately conveyed and users illiterate. Finally, workers are forced to bear the economic risks of business failures. When prices decline, when international markets deteriorate, the firms simply close down, or cut production--dismissing their employees, leaving them unemployed, confronted with starvation if they are landless.

International actors promote these kinds of agribusiness projects through loans and joint enterprise schemes with host governments. Often, however, the actual production is managed by a local subsidiary firm. This enables the international organizations, TNCs, and parastatal firms which have financed the enterprise to distance themselves from any legal accountability to workers. Indeed, local firms may also attempt to distance themselves by operating through "independent" intermediaries, by contracting with brokers and supervisors of labor for work to be done. Local officials regularly condone exploitation of workers by failing to enforce existing protective labor legislation, or by failing to report the need for it. Other local officials (perhaps with encouragement from higher-ups) help to conceal abuses and actively suppress formation of worker groups on the theory that these will disrupt the community.

(4) Exclusion and Repression:

In 1979 in Rome, the FAO-sponsored World Conference on Agrarian Reform and Rural Development enacted this declaration as its centerpiece resolution:

> Participation of the people in the institutions
> and systems which govern their lives is a basic
> human right and also essential for realignment of
> political power in favour of disadvantaged groups
> and for social and economic development. Rural
> development strategies can realize their full po-
> tential only through the motivation, active in-
> volvement and organization at the grassroots'
> level of rural people with special emphasis on
> the least advantaged strata, in conceptualizing
> and designing policies and programmes and in cre-
> ating administrative, social and economic insti-
> tutions including cooperative and other voluntary
> forms of organization for implementing and eval-
> uating them.

Development projects are regularly planned and executed through practices which subvert the policies promised in this declaration. Instead of securing the "basic right" of "participation," these practices promote exclusion which, in turn, leads to other impoverishing harms.

First, there are the practices of secrecy and *ex parte* decision making. Rarely do the rural poor play any meaningful role in the "conceptualization" and "design" of development programs. The various documents reflecting steps taken to initiate programs (studies, proposals, memoranda, etc.) are usually treated as confidential. Thus, the policy assumptions underlying a project, including assessments of its social costs and its impacts on target communities, are kept secret at the outset. While proposed projects may sometimes be described in national development plans, these documents

are singularly uninformative when it comes to detail. They
are neither directed at, nor circulated among, relevant
rural communities--who so often are potential victims of the
actions proposed; nor are plans published to invite consultation; rather they announce decisions already taken, confronting victim groups with a *fait accompli*. The formal agreements worked out between international and national actors
often do set out the details, including measures to be taken
in working with local peoples; hence they contain much of the
"law" governing implementation of a project. These agreements, too, are usually treated as state secrets. Cumulatively, these kinds of practices work to exclude effective
participation at the very stages where it may be needed most
if the object is to assure direct representation of affected
people so that they can identify their interests and secure
measures to protect them.

Second, there are practices of exclusion from, rather
than "participation" in, "institutions" and "systems" established to implement projects. Obviously the rural poor are
not included in the structure of the international organizations, "public" corporations, official agencies, and private
firms which, cumulatively, manage a development project. Nor
are there any established procedures providing access to
decision makers in these agencies. Rather such access is
systematically frustrated, often by imposing threats and
reprisals on those who seek it.

Third, various social conditions, practices, and procedures combine to insulate development actors from accountability for harms they inflict. The police and local officials are usually unsympathetic, often aligned with the harmdoers, often perpetrators of coercion to suppress complaints.

Administrative processes enabling victims to appeal to the heads of agencies with remedial powers are lacking. Access to the courts requires both organization and legal resources, and even where these exist there are other difficulties: judges who are unsympathetic or unprepared to take on such cases, lack of precedent and undeveloped civil remedies, hostile legal doctrines concerned with standing or jurisdiction or sovereign immunity, and other limitations on judicial power.

Fourth, are practices which frustrate organizations of the rural poor. The formation of self-managed participatory groups is obviously a prerequisite to any form of effective participation. The creation of effective organizations requires both grassroots activities (organizers, meetings, popular education) and assistance from outside groups to support these activities (including legal assistance). Contrary to both the letter and the spirit of the Rome declaration, these kinds of organizing activities are widely policed and repressed in most countries. Governments (notably local officials often acting at the behest of private actors) use a variety of legal measures: laws requiring licensing of associations and public meetings, or prohibitions against "seditious" activities and "threats to public order." Similar deterrents are used against those who try to mobilize "nongovernmental" support groups to work with the rural peoples.

International organizations are often in a position to promote popular participation. They initiate their own studies and other activities leading to the conceptualization and design of projects. These efforts may entail some consultation, but they rarely mobilize any genuine local participation in the sense of power-sharing. International organizations extend loans through agreements which may be the product of much negotiation, but local people are never made parties to these negotiations. They monitor implementation of projects and often conduct their own evaluations. These reports often expound the rhetoric of "participation"; they repeatedly find that projects have been inevitably flawed because it was lacking. Yet the agencies continue to condone the practices described above. Far from promoting popular participation, international development assistance practices often contribute to the erosion or further repression of this "basic right."

Failure to provide for participation leads to failures to calculate the social costs of projects, to reduce the risks inherent in them and limit potential damages and failure to compensate victims. Lack of participation also leads to failure to develop alternative, people-managed structures as vehicles for administering many kinds of development projects (such as water resource management or credit schemes), and the absence of these structures prevents effective administration of the project. The economic losses imposed on the poor as a result of denial of rights of participation are often serious enough. Perhaps even more serious, over the long haul, is the continuous fostering of governmental lawlessness and lack of accountability--the undermining of conditions necessary to promote recognition of human rights for the rural poor throughout the Third World.

Developing Strategies for Victim Groups

It may be relatively easy to identify, in general terms, basic interests of victim groups which must be protected when international development projects are initiated. For example, we can say that the land tenure rights of small-holders are essential to their welfare and must be protected. But it may be quite difficult to define with precision specific measures which should be demanded and which can be enforced efficiently enough to provide the necessary protections. (How are smallholder rights in land to be protected without overburdening an already complex land tenure situation--or without creating dependency on government bureaucracies?)

Thus, strategies for the poor must be context-specific and developed through their active participation as well as the participation of sympathetic specialists (e.g., in land tenure, economics, and the sociology of relevant communities) and lawyers equipped intellectually to respond to the challenges at hand.

(1) Combating Landlessness:

Perhaps the most urgent objective is to find ways to prohibit or regulate the variety of practices used by landlords, creditors, speculators, corporate agents, and others to force dispossession, or to secure transfers through deception.

Land alienation legislation prohibiting such transfers may provide one line of attack, particularly if it contains self-help remedies (providing for damages and equitable relief against violators). Land reform laws protecting rights of occupants may provide similar protections--or models for creating them. Historic tort and equitable remedies (e.g., actions to redress trespasses to land or physical security; actions to rescind unconscionable contracts) may provide other remedies. Legislation dealing with the administration

of "public" lands may also be an important target: the
power of government officials to lease--or license use of--
lands already occupied and used for self-support by smallholders must be sharply limited by according protections for
occupants similar to those accorded to other "tenants" under
land reform laws. The power to ignore occupants by declar-
ing their lands to be "vacant" can be limited by imposing
heavy burdens of proof before such declarations can be used
to transfer any rights in the land to people other than occupants. Again self-help remedies can be used to redress abuse
of these powers.

A second basic task may be to provide protections
against expropriation. Several protections seem important.
First, many expropriations are probably *ultra vires*: the
agency initiating the action may simply lack the power to
take the lands in question for the purposes announced; or it
may have failed to follow procedures which are a prerequisite
to any exercise of that power. Second, it should certainly
be a feature of the law governing expropriation that hearings
be held to enable prospective victims of the action to con-
test the value and necessity of the project proposed, to compel a weighing of the social costs of the project against the
benefits, to force consideration of alternative sites or at
least alterations in the project which will reduce the hardships inflicted. Third, the law governing any expropriation
should contain detailed procedures to assure both fair compensation and alternative homesites for those who must be
evicted. These procedures should make provision for establishing recognition of all possessory rights affected by the
taking--such as the independent possessory rights often enjoyed by wives in lands nominally held by their husbands.

The burden of proving these rights should be equitably allo-
cated--perhaps by creating participatory tribunals charged
with the task of mapping lands and identifying rights in
them. Again, using participatory processes, formulae for
compensation should be worked out in advance, and an adequate fund set aside to pay all anticipated claims.

As Smitu Kothari reports, these are the kinds of procedures which thousands of tribal people in India, the prospective victims of dam projects, have demanded; and their demands may well provide a model for other groups similarly
imperiled. Such guarantees provide the only way to assure
fairness to those threatened with landlessness. Moreover,
they force governments and international actors to calculate
and compensate many (though, of course, not all) of the social
costs which result from these kinds of development projects.

Self-help measures, generated through organizations of
victim groups are essential to these strategies. Through
group action, people can educate themselves in regard to the
nature of their tenures and the rights they may already possess and the measures they must demand to protect them. They
can form associations for self-protection purposes against
those who seek to force sales through threats of deception.
Groups can serve as entity trustees to secure recognition and
protection of the system of customs which governs tenures in
a particular locale. Groups usually provide the best, perhaps the only, way to resist governmental expropriations.
Similarly, if an expropriation proceeds, group participation
is essential to sort out and evaluate all the interests affected and to determine fair compensation. Groups provide
the most effective means, perhaps the only means, whereby
smallholders can gain access to the media to human rights

organizations and sympathetic elites, and, of course, to the courts.

(2) Combating Indebtedness:

Presumably, the basic objective is to secure access to credit necessary to meet *both* subsistence and cash crop farming needs--on terms which distribute both the risks of the loan and the costs of lending more equitably.

One set of protections may include: measures to prevent exaction of usurious interest rates; prohibitions against acceleration of repayment schedules; equitable remedies enabling rescission or revision of unconscionable contracts; tort remedies against creditors who use threats of violence and other unconscionable methods to coerce debtors. Debt relief measures can prohibit forfeiture of rights in land and of implements and animals necessary to cultivate it.

Another set of protections can focus on the need to reallocate the burden of the risks of crop or market failures for causes beyond the debtors' control. Debt relief measures can provide for moratoriums and rescheduling in such situations. Toward these ends low-cost insurance schemes can be developed, including funds to provide for disaster relief to cope with the vagaries of weather.

Again, collective self-help measures may be essential to create or enforce these protections. Participatory organizations also provide alternative institutions for allocating credit and administering collections and relief--provided, of course, that they are in fact self-managed.

(3) Combating Exploitation of Workers:

There are obviously many measures which can be developed to protect agrarian workers from the various kinds of exploitation we have noted. Indeed, there are dozens of ILO conventions which establish explicit protections against most abuses in order to protect those basic rights of agrarian workers set out in international conventions. There is no doubt that the world community has condemned all forms of exploitation, however ingenious; but the hard task is to devise more effective legal measures to secure the rights promised by these instruments.

Labor welfare legislation, dealing, for example, with wages and hours, hazardous and unhealthy work settings, and employment of women and child workers, is one approach. But the administration of these laws in various Philippine settings illustrates some of the pathologies that usually afflict bureaucracies charged with enforcement of these laws. Further, any legislation which relies on complaints and initiatives from exploited workers in order to trigger governmental investigations and administrative procedures and remedies is likely to go unenforced in many settings. Where workers are desperate to retain their employment, they will endure deprivation and abuse rather than risk unemployment as the cost of complaints and efforts to pressure bureaucrats to enforce the laws within their care.

Thus, it may be that new kinds of protections, addressed to the unhappy realities of the workers' situations, are necessary. These might take a variety of forms depending on the needs of particular groups. Penal sanctions, if sufficiently stringent, may provide better deterrents than laws which rely on civil or administrative remedies; at least penal sanctions provide a supplemental remedy urgently needed. Penal sanctions might be used to compel employers to uniformly observe certain basic conditions of employment (e.g., to observe minimum wages and various safety standards).

Parent companies can be held liable (in both civil and
criminal actions) for the abuses of subsidiary firms. Intermediaries who recruit or supervise employment of wage
workers can be policed by requiring that their activities
be both licensed and made subject to various kinds of controls. "Adhesion" contracts used by companies to employ
small farmers in production schemes can be regulated--and
indeed made subject to revision through invocation of equitable remedies. Insurance schemes can be required, whereby
companies must contribute to funds held in reserve to ameliorate the shock of business failures and the sudden unemployment of workers.

Another approach, a critical first step, must center on
strategies to provide worker education. Workers need to be
helped to understand their rights well, if they are to be
encouraged to risk attempts to enforce them.

Worker education underscores the importance of encouraging self-help measures through worker associations. At
the same time, the difficulty of forming such organizations
must be recognized. There are many different kinds of employment relationships--including full-time wage workers,
casual laborers, sharecroppers, farmers who produce under
putting-out schemes. Some of these categories are more vulnerable than others, and the difficulties of bringing people
together and forming effective organizations may vary considerably. All of this underscores the need to develop the
particular kinds of protections required in different settings to enable different kinds of rural workers to form
self-managed organizations and use them to pursue a variety
of objectives. These range from worker education, collective bargaining and self-help enforcement of protective

legislation and other rights (through both equitable and tort remedies), to the development of measures looking toward full worker participation in the management of these enterprises, and the creation of alternative structures and systems of production. Over the long haul, alternative participatory structures may provide the only appropriate vehicle to integrate cash crop production with people-centered development.

Developing Law and Legal Resources
for Victim Groups

A focus on law and legal resources is important. Of course, people who have been victimized by the combined actions of governmental bodies and powerful private actors often share a fundamental mistrust of law and legal institutions. They may choose to fight back by ignoring the law, or acting outside it. But such decisions entail risks, such as the risks of harsh, forcible retaliation against avowed lawbreakers, the risks of alienating supporters. By grounding their demands for protection and redress in law, those who fight back may be better able to mobilize support both within and without communities, to overcome inertia or fear. A "legal" analysis of group grievances helps to focus and clarify them. Finally, recourse to law in order to secure rights is a means not only of winning power for groups, but of institutionalizing it.

The task of developing law entails recourse to many different kinds of law: international law; tort and contract law; endogenous law derived from customs and widely shared values. The task of developing legal resources entails many activities, undertaken at both national and

international levels, ranging from grassroots projects
aimed at reciprocal education to provision of legal advocacy
for groups and the development of new kinds of legal expertise and professional skills. The processes of using law
and legal resources to empower and help victim groups may
entail recourse to the media and schools, to international
forums and diverse governmental bodies, as well as the courts.

Development actors use different kinds of law, instru-
mentally, to structure projects and immunize themselves from
accountability for harms inflicted. These usages of law
deserve critical analysis. International agreements; char-
ters of incorporation; legislation which delegates broad
discretionary powers to government agencies (including
powers to expropriate private lands and control public
lands); loan contracts between lenders and small farmers--
these are some of the forms of law used to structure development projects and arrogate powers to those who promote
them. Hoary doctrines of international law, "sovereignty
immunity," "state secrets," "standing," and others are in-
voked to shield official actors from accountability. Large
corporations immunize themselves by acting through local
subsidiaries or through other "independent contractors."
Local actors immunize themselves by coopting local agents of
law enforcement and administration, by invoking penal law to
deter opposition.

One task is to expose fundamental flaws in these usages
of law by showing how they are inconsistent with basic legal
principles, shared concepts of justice, the avowed objectives of national development policies--and universal rights
proclaimed by the international community. A second task is
to show how law, notably human rights law, can and should be

used as a means to identify, protect, and advance the basic
interests of the rural poor.

(1) Developing Law:

The human rights approach emphasizes the development of
human rights law as a basis for demanding various kinds of
protections against impoverishing harms; for imposing accountability on development actors; and for promoting participation, self-help projects, and alternative structures of
development.

a) *Developing Human Rights.* A growing body of international law can be used for these purposes: rights promised
by the Charter of the United Nations, the Universal Declaration of Human Rights, the International Covenants of Human
Rights, and numerous other international conventions promul-
gated through the UN system--notably by the world congresses
of the ILO--dealing with slavery, discrimination against and
exploitation of women and children, or the rights of rural
workers (including tenants, peasants, and other smallholders).
Other international declarations drawn up by world congresses
have focused on development isues and have repeatedly called
for recognition of the "basic right" of "participation" in
the development of agriculture and rural environments.

An essential purpose of many provisions in these instruments is to guarantee a wide range of basic rights deemed
essential to the welfare of the rural poor in Third World
countries. Prepared with the rural poor in mind, these provisions establish basic guarantees against practices which
render people landless; protections against creditors; protections for workers and peasants. They guarantee rights of
all people--but notably rural people--to food, education, and
health care. They guarantee rights of rural producers and

women to form self-managed organizations of their own
choice without any interference by organs of government.

Of course, the status of these rights as "positive law"
varies among countries. Some instruments have been ratified
by a significant number of Third World countries. Some important rights are incorporated into national constitutions
or legislation. Some are restated in the preambles or di-
rective principles of constitutions. Many have been reaf-
firmed in regional and international conventions and in
proclamations. All of these rights are said to reflect the
consensus of the world's peoples; and there can be little
doubt that they express values, needs, and aspirations of
impoverished peoples throughout the Third World--and thus
the needs of most of the world's people. The obligation of
international organizations to promote respect for these
rights is beyond question. So, we believe, is the obligation of other agencies which purport to engage in activities
affecting the lives and the welfare of the rural poor.

However, these rights can only gain life and significance when they are asserted for specific purposes and when
specific measures are developed to pursue those ends. The
essence of a right is the power to command the particular
protections necessary to secure the basic interests which
the right is supposed to secure. Since many of the most important universal human rights are expressed in general
terms (such as rights to "equality," "due process of law,"
"freedom of speech"), the processes of "rights development"
and recognition have often entailed three kinds of steps:
(i) asserting of the basic interests underlying the right;
(ii) demands for specific kinds of protections necessary in
the particular context to secure those interests; and (iii)

creation of procedures and structures which will assure
efficient implementation of these remedies. Thus, the
process of developing law for victim groups is, in part, a
process of developing particular component rights and remedial measures necessary to secure "basic," "universal"
rights promised by the world community. The process must
be context-specific: protections and remedies must be addressed to the particular kinds of wrongs to be addressed.

b) *Developing Specific Protections and Remedies*. Human rights scholars need to devote more attention to the
full range of different kinds of law implicated in these
strategies.

It is, for example, relatively meaningless to talk
about the "basic right" of "participation" unless one has in
mind the body of component rights and enforcement procedures
embodied in the right. Further, these protections must be
geared to the situation and needs of the beneficiaries of
the basic right. For people in some countries, "participation" may be realized through the right to vote, competitive
parties and elections, trade unions and interest groups, independent media and press freedoms--and access to the courts
to protect these institutions. To a peasant in Zaire, India,
or the Philippines the prospect is remote that he can realize much immediate power in these kinds of structures to protect basic interests which are imminently threatened. His
problem may center on finding other vehicles of participation
in order to secure access to credit, protect lands, and control the abuses of local officials and other elites.

Participation becomes valuable to victims and potential
victims when the right includes component rights to form self-
help groups and use them to secure rights to information,

rights of access to decision makers in relevant government agencies, rights to publicize grievances, rights of access to sympathetic and supportive organizations, rights of access to international organizations--and again access to the courts.

Measures needed to secure these protections may range over many legal fields: law governing voluntary associations, public meetings, and demonstrations; law governing access to government documents and opportunities to be heard in official forums; law governing the police. Penal sanctions and civil remedies for abuses of power are obviously important. Doctrines of sovereign immunity, "standing,' and other limitations on the capacity of courts to protect rights must be critiqued. Indeed, simple procedures to ensure direct access of aggrieved groups to the courts, to expedite hearings and overcome disadvantages such as illiteracy, language barriers, and other constraints may become an important part of the human rights agenda.

All this, of course, is only suggestive. We have focused on "participation" as an example of the kinds of challenges confronting those who would help develop law for the rural poor. In much the same way, specific remedies must be found to secure basic rights which protect smallholders, debtors, and workers, and which guarantee protection of food production and other essentials. Developing law to secure the "basic right" of "participation" may, however, be a useful point of departure. First, this right is widely recognized: devout lip service is repeatedly paid to the principle in official documents. Second, realization of the panoply of rights and remedies needed to secure participation is essential to empower people to assert and win other rights.

Indeed, the very processes of developing rights for victims must be participatory. It is not enough for scholars and other elites to discuss rights which should be accorded to the rural poor. Without the participation of concerned people, scholars often cannot know what rights are important in particular settings and what remedies are most feasible; and they certainly cannot bring those rights to life, for rights only come into a meaningful existence when they are understood and exercised by the intended beneficiaries.

(2) Developing Legal Resources:

Legal resources create the power to use law to protect and promote shared interests. Legal resources are created by mobilizing and aggregating the efforts of groups at both grassroots and other levels (including international levels), by generating and disseminating within these groups knowledge of relevant law and skills to use it; and by developing a wide variety of advocates and methods of advocacy. We focus here on a few illustrative tasks for support groups and supporters.

a) *Generating Knowledge*. This is a far bigger task than is often recognized. Ideally, there must be a conjuncture of efforts, undertaken in different settings, to identify and indeed create many different kinds of knowledge and skills.

At grassroots levels local groups must work together with supporters to generate the kinds of knowledge which help victims identify harms and harmdoers. Such knowledge also helps them to understand that they often have rights for preventing and redressing these activities, and to devise

strategies responsive to needs and relevant to circum-
stances--notably self-managed, self-help strategies.

Knowledge of law *relevant to the needs* of these protag-
onists must also be generated: it does not often exist *a
priori* any more than does some other kind of knowledge, such
as knowledge of local agronomy of local health needs.

Consider, for example, the task of creating knowledge
of the law governing the rights of victims and supporters to
organize collective self-help activities. In few countries
have many lawyers addressed themselves to this subject.
There are, of course, many different kinds of legal constraints which governments can impose on these activities;
but the degree to which such constraints are used may vary.
Conversely, the extent to which rights of association for
various purposes are protected may also vary. Such rights
may be protected in broad terms by national constitutions,
or at least in relation to organizing trade unions, cooperatives, educational bodies, or other specific kinds of
groups. Some countries have ratified ILO Convention 141--or
announced their intention to do so. This convention (and
other ILO and UN instruments) contains, broad, emphatic guarantees on the rights of rural workers, smallholders, tenants,
and rural women to form self-managed organizations, free from
licensing requirements or similar kinds of interference.
Knowledge of how these sources of law, and perhaps the resources of the ILO, can be used to demand protection of
rights to organize may be crucial. All these strands of
knowledge help people form appropriate strategies for organizational activities. They also begin to reveal an important
part of the agenda for human rights groups, national and international, who become concerned with the plight of the

rural poor.

That is simply one illustration of knowledge-generation tasks which call for efforts by sympathetic lawyers and others. It shows that lawyers who care can supply various forms of help which few lawyers have yet provided--perhaps because their whole professional training and orientation has never focused on the kinds of problems we are addressing here. Similarly, few if any lawyers have ever written critiques of the legal regimes governing rural credit and indebtedness in their country, or critiques of legal regimes governing expropriation. In similar ways, lawyers and others working in international NGOs can contribute valuable knowledge to aid efforts at local and national levels: the legal accountability of TNCs, the World Bank, and other IOs to international human rights law is an important subject--
particularly if it is addressed from the perspective of victims.

b) *Developing Advocacy*. While the term often connotes visions of the forensic efforts of lawyers in tribunals, advocacy can be seen simply as an extension of the educational efforts described above: the legal resources' approach (as distinguished from conventional "legal services" approaches) calls for many kinds of education/persuasion efforts addressed to a wide variety of targets (in addition to courts), asserted in a wide variety of forums (national and international) by a wide variety of advocates (group leaders, community paralegals, lawyers, scholars, religious leaders, and many others).

The tasks of developing advocacy for (and by) victim peoples may include activities as the following:

(a) preparing pamphlets and educational materials, documentary films, and other kinds of reports aimed at particular audiences;

(b) preparing submissions to investative commissions or legislation committees or international conferences;

(c) organizing workshops for lawyers, judges, media people, and other influential elites;

(d) organizing protest activities, not only locally, but in other nerve-center places; and

(e) advocacy to forge networks and concerted action programs for church groups, foundations, human rights organizations, and others.

Advocacy efforts at regional and international levels--perhaps conducted under the aegis of prestigious NGOs and, if possible, UN agencies--may be particularly important because in so many countries there is so much repression at local levels.

Strategic Action Campaigns

Occasionally some tragic event occurs (the Bhopal disaster is a glaring example) which attracts media attention and public concern toward the victims of wrongdoing by participants in international development projects. At least widespread feelings of shock, desire to help, and the sense of injustice generated by such events can provide the occasion and energy (too seldom seized) for social activists to mobilize a broad range of groups and projects with, and in behalf of, those already harmed and those threatened by similar disaster.

These efforts, sometimes called "strategic action campaigns," have been attempted in India, notably in the wake of Bhopal. They entail initiatives to organize *concerted* action by a number of different kinds of concerned professionals, social action groups (e.g., environmental, health, human rights), and grassroots organizations.

One step is to develop, share, and disseminate knowledge of the activity--the harms it has inflicted (or threatens) and the social impact and cost of these harms; wrongful practices associated with the activity which causes these harms or which, in other ways, violate the human rights of those threatened by the activity; law relevant to the governance and accountability of those who manage the activity, and legal remedies of people injured or threatened by it; and other measures which can be undertaken to prevent these outcomes (and strategies to secure them).

Thus, "strategic action campaigns" have been directed at generating and sharing knowledge which different kinds of groups and concerned professionals can use to induce more focused, reinforcing action--e.g., the media; influential persons in differing professional circles; courts, legislative bodies, and other agencies which have powers to impose accountability for wrongdoing; international organizations which can influence the development of law governing the activity.

The Narmada project in India, described by Smitu Kothari, provides an illustration of the need for this kind of mobilization. The government of the State of Gujarat (acting through various ministries in collaboration with agencies of the government of India, the World Bank, and other international assistance agencies) has decided to

build a dam to generate power for various urban industrial
centers and to develop irrigated farming. The dam sites,
and the lakes they will produce, will destroy many square
miles of forest areas, parts of which are inhabited by many
thousands of tribal people who have lived in (and in harmony with) forest environments for centuries. These environments are the source of their culture and way of life,
as well as their subsistence.

The victims of the project and their allies have, with
limited resources at their command, sought to educate various
sectors of the public about their plight. They have raised
a number of different kinds of issues which deserve widespread and intensive attention.

First are the claims that the harms and social costs
which will be produced by the project far outweigh its benefits. They believe the dam will prove to be (as others in
India have) a technological disaster which will produce other
disasters: the river and the ecology of the region will produce silting which will fill up the dam basin, causing further flooding and ultimate failure of the project. They believe the project will destroy more of India's deteriorating
forest lands, a heritage which can never be replaced and so
must now be protected with special care. They believe that
while the dam will bring benefits to some--e.g., trees for
industries, irrigation for large-scale farmers and power for
urban consumers who can afford it--the project will inflict
costs on many others who must be made to bear these burdens
while those who gain will risk and suffer nothing. They believe it is wrong to resolve these issues through convoluted
processes of decision making which exclude participation of
people most directly affected--the tribals. They believe

that the case of the Narmada project is not an isolated extreme example; it is but part of a pattern [of "development"] which is very rapidly stabilizing itself in our country and perhaps others where the rulers are by and large not accountable to the people at large. At this point hopes for halting the project altogether are dim.

A *second set of claims* relates to the combined failure of all of those responsible for financing and "implementing" the project to provide compensatory justice to the many who will be seriously injured by it. These grievances have led to demonstrations by thousands of potential "victims" at the dam site headquarters--a kind of activity which is "unprecedented" in this region.

Underlying these protests were demands for assurances-- "law"--which will enable families ousted from their historic homelands:

   a) to secure *fair* compensation for lands expropriated from them;

   b) to secure (through purchase, at affordable prices, and not coerced exchange) at least five acres per family of similar forest land for resettlement--and to secure stable titles to these new lands;

   c) to secure protection from outside land speculators who are already trying to exploit the prospect of landless people seeking new home sites;

   d) to secure *fair* compensation for other costs inevitably inflicted on each ousted family as it seeks to move to and resettle in a new environment; and

   e) to secure recognition of formulas which will enable calculation with some certainty (for

> each family) of all of these costs, and thus
> formulas which will generate adequate budget
> allocations in advance to meet these costs.
> (At present only 250 million rupees have
> been appropriated for rehabilitation of all
> of the potential victims--and the total num-
> ber of them has never, apparently, been of-
> ficially estimated. By way of contrast, 450
> million rupees have been appropriated for
> the housing of several hundred staff at the
> dam site headquarters.)

In response to these claims, the people (like countless other victim groups in similar situations) have received *verbal* assurances by various high-ranking officials (e.g., Gujarat's Minister of Irrigation) that their claims (or many of them) will be met, justice will be done. Any lawyer worth his/her salt could readily know that none of these officials have the "jurisdiction" to carry out these kinds of prom-ises--assuming the officials will still be around when the promise comes due.

A third set of claims relates to the accountability of international organizations, notably the World Bank, which are partners in this project. Is it legal for the Bank to finance projects which will clearly violate human rights pro-tected by both national and international human rights guar-antees--for example, the Constitution of India, the Universal Declaration, and the UN Covenants? Should not the Bank in-sist, from the very beginning, that this (or any) project will be carried forward in strict compliance with this law? Should not the Bank put itself under law by prescribing pro-cedures, to be followed at every stage of a project, which will assure protection of those rights which international law holds to be "universal"--and presumably binding on inter-national organizations?

These are only some of the issues. Underlying them is a deeper concern. *There is no law*—at least none yet known to the Narmada victims and those helping them—which is recognized by the agencies financing and building the dam and which explicitly addresses the concerns set forth above.

Thus, the Narmada project has provided a clear example of a tragedy which should, even in this age of grand-scale human suffering, anger those with an operative sense of injustice. Effective reaction to this kind of situation calls for the enlistment of many different kinds of social activists and professionals—a pooling of knowledge from environmentalists, economists, engineers, and many others—notably lawyers. The hope is that in the future these skills can be mobilized in order to make "economic development" more consonant with social justice.